40

iPod

TECHNIQUES

ISBN: 981-05-3721-2

Printed and bound in the Republic of Korea.

How to contact us

support@youngjin.com
feedback@youngjin.com.sg
Fax: 65-6339-1403

Credits

Authors: Troy Silver, Rand Miranda
Production Editor: Patrick Cunningham
Editor: Elisabeth Beller
Indexer: Steven Rath
Book and Cover Designer: Litmus

Cover Photo courtesy of Apple Computer, Inc.

40

iPod

TECHNIQUES

Y.

C o n t e n t s

Introduction | **Say Hello to Your Little Friend**   **6**

    The iPod Phenomenon   8

    Buying an iPod   10

    Mac vs. Windows   11

    Installing Software   13

    Getting Started in iTunes   16

Chapter 1 | **Getting Started**   **24**

  01 Your Battery and You   26

  02 Getting to Know Your iPod   29

  03 Customizing Your iPod Settings   32

  04 iPod, Meet iTunes   35

  05 Organizing Your Library   37

  06 Creating Playlists in iTunes   41

  07 Automatic Sync   45

  08 Semi-Automatic Sync   47

  09 Transferring Audio Manually   49

  10 On-the-Go Playlists   51

  11 Transcoding Audio   53

Chapter 2 | **Expanding Your Audio Collection**   **56**

  12 Exploring the iTunes Music Store   58

  13 Heard Any Good Books Lately?   61

  14 Podcasts   64

  15 Free Music, the Lawful Way   68

Chapter 3 | **Beyond Audio—iPod Extras**   **70**

  16 Clocks   72

  17 Contacts   75

  18 Calendars   78

  19 Notes and Voice Memos   81

  20 Extra Extras—The iPod Nano   83

  21 Third-Party Software   86

Chapter 4 | **One Hard Drive, to Go**   **90**

  22 Using the iPod as a Portable Hard Drive   92

  23 Transferring Your iTunes Library to Another Computer   94

Chapter 5 | Photos on the Run   96

24   Transferring Photos to and from Your iPod   98
25   Viewing Photos on Your iPod   101
26   Connecting Your iPod to Your TV   103
27   Using the iPod with a Digital Camera   105

Chapter 6 | Do the Shuffle   108

28   Welcome to the Shuffle   110
29   Advanced Shuffle Operations   113
30   Using the Shuffle as a Flash Drive   116

Chapter 7 | Accessories Make the iPod   118

31   A Case for Cases   120
32   Headphones   124
33   Stereo Docks   128
34   Car Stereo Hookups   131
35   Add-Ons and Upgrades   134

Chapter 8 | Maintenance and Troubleshooting   138

36   Backing Up Your iPod   140
37   Solutions for Common Problems   143
38   Restoring Your iPod   146
39   Keeping Your Software Up to Date   147
40   Physical Care of Your iPod   151

Chapter 9 | The Fifth-Generation iPod and iTunes 6   154

iPod Advancements   156
Feature Comparison and Basic Operations   156
Unique 5G iPod Operations   157
Filling Your iPod with Videos   158
New in iTunes 6   159

Index   162

40 iPod Techniques

Say Hello to Your Little Friend

An iPod is an inviting thing; it wants you to want it. Apple designed their little moneymaker to simply work-without a hassle. However, they also designed the iPod to offer a robust assortment of features, and in so doing have complicated matters for a few would-be iPod junkies. This, of course, is where 40 iPod Techniques comes in.

We'll begin with a short introduction to the world of the iPod, including a brief history of the iPod empire, tips for buying an iPod, differences between using one on a Windows PC and a Mac, and instructions for setting up iTunes (your iPod's best friend). In subsequent chapters we'll move on to the iPod's more advanced features, but for now we'll stick to the basics.

Note that, although the various iPods-iPod, iPod Nano, iPod Mini, and iPod Shuffle-differ in their features and operations, we've endeavored to address all iPod models. Windows users and Mac users will find directions specific to their operating systems when procedures differ between the two.

The iPod Phenomenon

Introduction

As the proud owner of an iPod, you're no doubt aware of the revolution that has taken place in digital music over the last several years. The convergence of Internet technologies with compressed audio formats and advancements in portable hardware have given way to a new era in the distribution of music. The ways in which we find, pay for, and acquire music are changing fundamentally. Perhaps even the way we think of music has changed. Arguably, there is no greater symbol of this "new way" than the iPod.

A quick look at the iPod's history, however, might surprise you. The device's beginnings were ever so humble, and its near-single-handed ignition of the MP3 player revolution was far from predictable.

The first-generation (1G) iPod debuted in 2001. It featured a mere 5 gigabytes (GB) of storage and a price point of $399 (Appalling, isn't it?). It was met with understandable skepticism by the press, but—astonishingly—was a hit with consumers. Apple quickly followed up with a 10 GB model priced at $499.

Apple released its second-generation (2G) iPod in 2002. In addition to bumping up capacities to 10 and 20 GB, Apple refined the iPod's control scheme to include a touch-sensitive control wheel. Variations on this mechanism have been featured in every iPod since (with the exception of the iPod Shuffle). 2G models were priced at $399 and $499.

The third-generation (3G) iPod debuted in 2003. Eventually, models were released in 10, 15, 20, 30, and 40 GB sizes. Refinements to the unit's design and interface, mixed with a brilliant marketing campaign (i.e., Apple's famous "silhouette" commercials), gave birth to the iPod phenomenon. At this point Apple's device became a must-have item for so many of us. This was hardly the end of the iPod's development, however.

▲ First-generation (1G) iPod

▲ Second-generation (2G) iPod

▲ Third-generation (3G) iPod

Apple revealed a new kind of iPod in early 2004—the iPod Mini. By using "micro" hard drives, these units traded song capacity for a smaller, more stylish form factor. The first-generation Mini came in five colors: blue, gold, green, pink, and silver. The Mini also introduced the Click Wheel, Apple's ultimate refinement of their hardware interface. (The Click Wheel is still featured in Apple's current iPod lineup.) Priced at $249 for 4 GB of storage, the Mini was largely dismissed by the press as too expensive, but consumers failed to notice; units sold so fast that Apple had difficulty meeting demand.

▲ iPod Mini, in pink

In mid-2004, Apple unveiled its fourth-generation (4G) iPod. The 4G iPod came in 20 and 40 GB capacities, and adopted the Mini's now-famous Click Wheel interface. Substantial improvements to battery life were also featured. Models were priced at $299 and $399.

The iPod Photo (or Color iPod) emerged in late 2004. Featuring a color screen, this iteration of Apple's device was capable of storing and displaying digital photos in numerous file formats. It originally came in 40 and 60 GB capacities, priced at $499 and $599, respectively.

Late 2004 also brought us the iPod U2 Special Edition. Cased in black with a red Click Wheel, the unit came with U2's latest album (*How to Dismantle an Atomic Bomb*) preloaded. It also featured engravings of the band members' signatures (on its chrome back plate) and a $50 gift certificate good toward the purchase of a U2 box set at Apple's iTunes Music Store.

▲ Fourth-generation (4G) color iPod

This brings us to 2005 and the glorious present. The 4G iPod and the iPod Photo have merged; 20 and 60 GB models each feature color screens with digital photo support. The iPod U2 Special Edition has also seen improvements; it now features the same hardware found in the latest iPods, as well as a lower price. We've also seen the emergence of the iPod Shuffle, a flash-based device that trades features and capacity for a rock-bottom price and a tiny footprint. As for the Mini, it saw its second generation—featuring 6 GB of storage, longer battery life, and enhanced case colors—only to be discontinued in favor of Apple's latest achievement: the iPod Nano. The Nano essentially combines the best features of all the other iPods, the flash-based memory of the Shuffle (with a capacity comparable to the Mini's), and the color screen (with photo support) of the full-size iPod. All this comes, of course, in an absurdly small size.

If the history of the iPod teaches us anything, it's that portable audio technology is moving at a breakneck pace. The innovation expressed in the evolution of the iPod can only mean one thing: the iPod of the future will blow your mind. But that's no reason not to enjoy the iPod of the present! Let's have a look at your new best friend.

▲ iPod Nano, in black

Buying an iPod

If you don't already own an iPod, a few basic facts may assist your purchase. For starters, Apple maintains strict pricing control over all their products. As a result, the benefits of bargain hunting are largely negated; with rare exception, your iPod will cost exactly what Apple says it should cost. You can always venture into the vast cornucopia that is eBay (http://www.ebay.com) and take your chances, but the iPod is a fairly expensive device in a small, fragile package—you never know what you'll get. Furthermore, a warranty is your iPod's best friend, and a warranty might be difficult to acquire through an auction.

The iPod has survived one or two hardware deficiencies in its day, and its battery in particular has been a source of much anxiety. To address these concerns, Apple offers a one-year limited warranty. The small print for Apple's warranty can be found on their Web site (http://www.apple.com/legal/warranty/ipodisight.html). Apple also has a policy governing battery replacements. For details, visit the relevant page on their site: http://www. apple.com/batteries/replacements.html. You have the option of purchasing Apple's extended warranty, which adds a year to your coverage period, when you buy your iPod.

If you're truly paranoid—quite understandable given the delicate nature of the iPod—you can purchase warranties through third parties. Major electronics chains typically offer their own warranty protections (for a fee) at the point of purchase. It is for this reason that shopping around might be wise; often these third-party warranties offer solutions that are more straightforward and convenient than Apple's policy.

A final word of warning: the Web has allowed for the proliferation of unauthorized resellers. These are online stores that are not authorized by product manufacturers to sell their products. Often these stores sell unauthorized products at lower prices, but there is a catch: manufacturers typically void the warranties for products sold through unauthorized resellers. In general, it's best to play it safe and confirm that your iPod source is authorized by Apple to sell iPods. If not, be sure the store you purchase from offers their own warranty protection. The last thing you want is a $399 paperweight!

Mac vs. Windows

In the iPod's younger days, it was necessary to purchase an iPod pre-formatted for use on either Windows or Mac computers. Fortunately, Apple has come a long way toward unifying the iPod experience.

WARNING: Though your iPod will happily work on either Windows PCs or Macs, there are limitations to its cross-platform operability. iPods formatted for use on PCs may be connected to Macs. iPods formatted for use on Macs, however, require the use of third-party software to operate on PCs. By default, if you connect a Mac-formatted iPod to a PC, you will receive a prompt indicating that you must reformat your iPod for use with the Windows operating system. (Note that formatting your iPod will delete its contents.)

iTunes, the program that controls your iPod on your computer, is nearly identical for both Windows and Mac users. The look, feel, and navigation are almost indistinguishable. The only substantive difference between versions lies in their use of third-party plug-ins (i.e., small programs that can be installed to add to iTunes' functionality). In short, the plug-ins you can get for the Windows version of iTunes differ from those that are available on the Mac.

iTunes for Windows is also capable of converting Windows Media Audio (WMA) files into alternate file formats; the WMA format isn't supported in the Mac version.

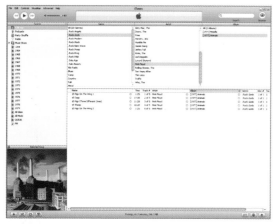

▲ iTunes for Windows PC

▲ iTunes for Mac OS X

This isn't to say there aren't legitimate differences between the Windows and Mac user experiences. Once you move beyond the protective confines of Apple's iTunes software, these differences emerge.

For instance, depending on the age of your computer, a PC is more likely to support USB 2.0 connectivity, while a Mac is more likely to support FireWire connectivity. There are also procedural differences when using your iPod as an external hard drive (these will be covered later in the book). Most importantly, Apple provides a suite of software tools that automate many of the non-music features of your iPod. Photos, contacts, and calendar events can all be synced automatically using Apple's iPhoto, Address Book, and iCal programs, respectively. However, these programs are only available to Mac users. PC users can still enjoy these features, but they must use third-party software to unlock the full potential of their iPods.

▲ iPhoto, Apple's digital photo application

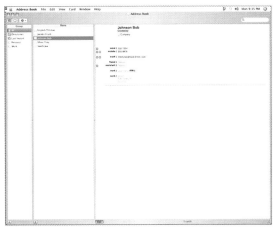
▲ Address Book, Apple's contacts application

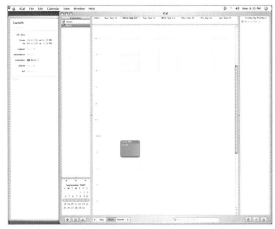
▲ iCal, Apple's calendar application

Where applicable, we will provide alternate information for Windows and Mac users. We'll also point you toward third-party software that can improve the functionality of your iPod. Before we do that, however, let's take a look at the software that will get your iPod up and running on your computer.

Installing Software

There are two pieces of software you'll need to operate your iPod: iPod Updater, which keeps your iPod's internal software up to date, and iTunes, the music program through which you'll fill your iPod with files. If you're a Mac user running OS X, you almost certainly have both pieces of software installed already; they're installed by default with OS X and are pre-loaded on new Macs running OS X. (However, this software may be out of date on your computer.) If you're running a Windows machine, you will need to install the necessary software manually. Installation instructions for both platforms are included here.

Power User's Tip
Although the instructions provided here refer to the installation disc that came with your iPod, this software may be outdated right out of the box. It depends entirely on how long your iPod spent on a shelf before you snatched it up. To check for software updates, refer to Technique 39 in this book.

Mac OS X Software Installation

1. Insert the CD that came with your iPod in your CD or DVD drive.

2. Double-click the iPod CD icon that appears on your desktop.

3. Double-click the iPod Installer folder that appears in the iPod CD window.

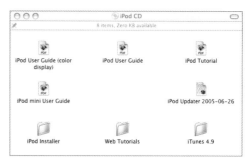

4. Double-click the iPod.mpkg icon that appears in the iPod Installer window.

5. Follow the prompts to install iPod Updater.

6. Return to the iPod CD window and click the iTunes folder (the version number will differ depending on when you purchased your iPod).

7. Click the icon with the .mpkg extension to launch the iTunes installer.

8. Follow the installer steps to install iTunes.

Windows Software Installation

1. Insert the CD that came with your iPod in your CD or DVD drive.

2. When the Choose Setup Language dialog box appears, select your preferred language and click OK.

3. When the InstallShield Wizard completes its work, follow the on-screen prompts to install iPod Updater.

4. After restarting your computer (keeping the installation disc in your drive), select My Computer from the Start menu.

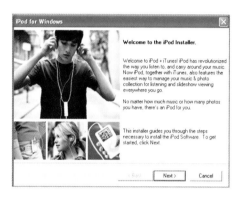

5. Right-click the iPod CD icon and select Explore from the pop-up menu.

6. In the iPod CD window, select Program Files > Apple > iTunes, then the folder corresponding to your preferred language. Finally, click the iTunesSetup icon to begin the installation process.

7. Once the InstallShield Wizard completes its work, follow the on-screen prompts to install iTunes.

Getting Started in iTunes

With your software installed, it's time to explore iTunes. Though it's possible to move audio to and from your iPod without iTunes (using third-party programs), Apple designed iTunes with the iPod in mind, so it's unlikely you'll find another solution as elegant. To get started, launch iTunes and familiarize yourself with the user interface.

A. **iTunes menu (Mac only)**: Mac users can set their iTunes preferences and quit iTunes from this menu.

B. **File menu**: Create playlists, import audio, or export library data.

C. **Edit menu**: Select interface/display preferences here. Windows users can change their iTunes preferences here.

D. **Controls menu**: Set the repeat-play mode, turn shuffle play on and off, change the playback volume, or eject a disk from your CD/DVD drive.

E. **Visualizer menu**: Turn on and set the size for the iTunes Visualizer.

F. **Advanced menu**: Switch to mini-player mode, subscribe to podcasts, access track information on the Internet, and control digital rights management (DRM).

G. **Window menu (Mac only)**: Mac users can control the iTunes window from here—Minimize, Zoom, etc.

H. **Help menu**: Select from a variety of help and Internet-related functions.

I. **Transport and volume controls**: Control playback and adjust volume here. Click and hold the forward and back buttons to fast-forward or rewind, respectively.

J. **Sound animation button**: This button appears when a track is playing. Click the arrow icon to change the now-playing display to an animation based on the sound frequencies of the currently playing track. (This is separate from iTunes' Visualizer feature.)

K. **Track info and progress display**: Displays information for the currently playing track. The name of the current track is displayed at the top. Click the text below to toggle between the album title and artist name (the display will cycle between these automatically during playback). Elapsed time is always displayed to the left of the progress bar. By default, the total track time is displayed to the right of the progress bar. Click the total time to switch its display to time remaining. Click (or click and drag) the progress bar to jump to any spot in the currently playing track.

L. **Return to currently playing track button**: If you browse your library while playing a track, click this button to select the currently playing track in your iTunes browser.

M. **Search field**: Enter search criteria to search your library. After entering a search criteria, iTunes 5.0 (or later) will reveal the Search Bar, which allows you to narrow your search results by pressing a series of categorized buttons.

N. **Contextual button**: Depending on your activity in iTunes, this button will change between several quick tasks—Browse, Burn CD, Import, Options, and Refresh.

O. **Source list**: Select from the various categories of audio supported by iTunes. Playlists are stored here, and your iPod will appear here when it's connected to your computer.

P. **Selected Song/Now Playing frame**: Click the frame title bar to toggle between displaying the album art for the currently selected song or the currently playing song.

Q. **Browser frame**: When the browser is open, select tracks through a hierarchical scheme—genre, then artist, then album title. Individual track listings appear in the Track frame below.

R. **Track frame**: Select audio tracks here. Double-click tracks to play them. Drag and drop tracks to add them to playlists in the Source list. Right-click (or Ctrl-click) tracks to select secondary options and change track information (via the Get Info selection). Select multiple tracks by holding down the Command key (Mac) or the Ctrl key (PC). Select a range of tracks by selecting the first track in the range, holding down the Shift key, and selecting the final track in the range. Right-click (or Ctrl-click) the column titles to hide or display columns representing the various informational tags of your tracks. Click and drag entire columns to arrange their order to your liking. Resize columns by clicking and dragging their outer edges. Auto size columns by double-clicking their outer edges. Auto size all the columns by right-clicking (or Ctrl-clicking) a column title and selecting the Auto Size All Columns option.

S. **iTunes Music Store search button**: If the "Show links to Music Store" option is selected in your iTunes preferences (it is by default), the music store link button appears next to each track. Click the button to automatically search for related music at the iTunes Music Store (iTMS).

T. **Create a playlist button**: Click to create a new playlist. Hold down the Option button (Mac) or Shift button (PC) to create a smart playlist.

U. **Turn shuffle on or off button**: Toggle shuffle play for the currently selected tracks or playlist. (Shuffle play parameters can be adjusted in your iTunes preferences.)

V. **Playlist repeat mode button**: Toggle between playing tracks once, repeating all the tracks in the current playlist, or repeating a single track.

W. **Show or hide song artwork button**: Click to show or hide the Selected Song/Now Playing frame, which displays album artwork.

X. **Totals display**: Shows the total number of tracks, combined time, and combined file size for the tracks currently displayed in the Track frame. Click the display to switch the time given from a decimal value to the hours-minutes-seconds format.

Y. **Open the Equalizer window button**: Click to open iTunes' built-in sound equalizer. (Equalizer settings attached to individual tracks will transfer to your iPod.)

Z. **Turn visual effects on or off button**: Click to turn on the Visualizer, which displays animated visual effects that react to the currently playing track. Hold down the Option key (Mac) or Shift key (PC) to change this button so that it activates the full-screen Visualizer option.

AA. **Eject disc button**: Click to eject the disc in your CD/DVD drive.

It is beyond the scope of this book to fully explore the functionality of iTunes, but there are a few basics that are critical to your iPod experience.

mporting Audio into iTunes

Obviously, the most important feature of iTunes is its ability to store music that you can transfer to your iPod. Of course, to do that, you must first add music to your library. iTunes provides a number of options for starting your collection of tracks.

▶ ▶ ▶ A Quick Guide to Audio Formats

Before you begin work on your track library, it's important to understand the fundamentals of the digital audio formats supported by iTunes. To begin, there are two primary categories of audio formats:

Lossless (AIFF, Apple Lossless, WAV, etc.): Lossless audio files offer perfect reproduction of the original CD sound; no sound data is "thrown away" to facilitate file compression. Lossless formats sound identical to the original recordings they're ripped from, but their file sizes tend to be very large compared to lossy audio formats.

Lossy (AAC, MP3, WMA. etc.): Lossy audio formats discard sound data in the interest of reducing file size. These audio tracks do not sound as good as the CD tracks they're ripped from, but their file sizes are extraordinarily small. For portable audio devices such as the iPod (which feature significantly less storage capacity than your computer's hard drive), lossy audio formats are still very much required if you want to maximize the number of songs on your player. Audio quality and file size are determined by the specific file format used and the encoding settings used to compress the original CD track. Generally speaking, the higher the bit rate, the better the sound (and the larger the file).

iTunes supports a number of audio formats in both lossless and lossy formats. Lossy tracks can be encoded at a variety of bit rates. See the following descriptions for a brief primer:

AAC (Lossy): Sometimes called MP4, Apple's AAC audio format is widely considered to offer superior sound quality (at comparable encoding settings) to traditional MP3 audio. The AAC format also allows for the DRM system used by Apple to protect music purchased through the iTMS; this prevents users from copying and trading music tracks. We recommend AAC at a bit rate of 128 kbps as the format of choice for your iPod, as this combines solid audio quality with small file sizes. Tracks purchased through the iTMS are encoded in this format, and these tracks are generally perceived to be "CD quality."

AIFF (Lossless): AIFF is the standard uncompressed, lossless audio format for Macintosh computers. With their introduction of the Apple Lossless format, Apple essentially made the AIFF format obsolete (at least, as far as iTunes and your iPod are concerned).

Apple Lossless (Lossless): Apple Lossless (AL) is the newest addition to the list of audio formats supported in iTunes. It combines the sonic benefits of lossless audio with a moderate level of file compression (to reduce file size). On average you can expect files sizes to be two-thirds of their original size on CD. We recommend importing audio into iTunes using this format—if you have the hard-drive space. By converting CDs to the AL format you create a perfect reproduction of the original disc, which can then be archived or converted to other (lossy) audio formats, depending on your needs. Using AL for your iTunes library can complicate the use of your iPod; see Technique 11, which deals with transcoding audio formats, for additional details.

MP3 (Lossy): The MP3 format is the most widely used audio format. Although alternate methods for encoding MP3s exist, and the format is still quite viable (when compared to Apple's newer AAC format), the MP3 encoder used by iTunes is widely judged to be of poor quality. For most users, Apple's AAC encoder is preferable. Unless you plan to use your iTunes library to supply audio tracks to non-iPod devices (which do not support the AAC format), we do not recommend encoding files in the MP3 format.

WAVE (Lossless): The WAVE format is the Windows equivalent of Apple's AIFF format. This is a lossless—but uncompressed—audio format. Again, there's very little reason to use this format now that the AL format offers lossless audio quality with file compression.

WMA (Lossy): The WMA format is a creation of Microsoft and offers solid audio quality with impressive file compression. It is a lossy format, and you can think of it as Microsoft's version of Apple's AAC format. iTunes and the iPod do not support the WMA format, but the Windows version of iTunes will offer to convert WMA files into a supported format if you drag them into the iTunes Track frame.

WARNING: The process of converting a file from one audio format to another is called transcoding. Note that transcoding from a lossy format into any other audio format will dramatically reduce the quality of the audio track.

Transcoding should only be considered when using lossless source files. It is for this reason that we recommend encoding your audio in the AL format, as these tracks can be converted to any lossy format without a reduction in sound quality.

▶ ▶ ▶ Importing Audio from Your Hard Drive

The first time you run iTunes, the iTunes Setup Assistant will give you the option of automatically importing any audio tracks (in supported audio formats) currently on your hard drive. If you prefer, you can do this manually by clicking and dragging audio files from your computer's drive directory into the iTunes Track frame. When adding audio tracks in this manner, you have the option of leaving the tracks in their current locations or having iTunes consolidate them by copying them into the library location specified in your iTunes preferences. To toggle this choice, follow these steps:

1. Select Preferences from the iTunes (Mac) or Edit (PC) menu.

2. Select the Advanced tab from the Preferences window.

3. Toggle the "Copy files to iTunes Music folder when adding to library" option according to your preference.

▶ ▶ ▶ Importing Audio from a CD

If you're new to music on your computer, it's likely that most of the music destined for your iPod will come from your CD collection. Once you've decided on an audio format for iTunes and your iPod, enter your iTunes preferences to select your desired audio import options.

1. Select Preferences from the iTunes (Mac) or Edit (PC) menu.

2. Select the Importing tab.

3. Select your preferred audio format from the Import Using pull-down menu.

4. Select your import settings from the Setting pull-down menu. Presets are provided for each audio format, or select Custom from the pull-down menu to manually tailor your settings. Generally speaking (for lossy audio formats), the higher the bit rate the better the sound, and the larger the file size. Consult your iTunes documentation for additional details related to import settings.

With your import settings properly configured, use the following procedure to add CD tracks to your iTunes library.

1. Insert a CD in your CD/DVD drive.

2. A CD icon, as well as the title of your disc, will appear in the iTunes Source list. Click this icon to display the tracks from your disc in the Track frame.

3. By default, all the tracks will be selected for importing (selected tracks show a checked box to the left of their names). To deselect tracks, simply click the desired check boxes to remove their checks.

4. The contextual button at the upper right of the iTunes window now reads "Import." Click this button to import the selected tracks. Alternatively, select your desired tracks in the Track frame, right-click (or Ctrl-click) one of the highlighted tracks, and select "Convert Selection to [currently selected import format]" from the pop-up menu.

5. iTunes will begin the conversion process for the selected tracks. The primary iTunes display changes to show progress information.

When the conversion process is finished, you may eject your CD—your music has been encoded and saved to your computer! We'll share some helpful techniques related to what you can do with your imported audio tracks later in the book, but for now let's get down to business; it's time to take a good look at your iPod.

40 iPod Techniques

Getting Started

In Chapter 1 we'll acquaint you with the basics of your iPod. First, we'll familiarize you with your iPod's hardware and software. We'll then discuss working in iTunes and connecting your iPod to your computer. We'll close out Chapter 1 with some advanced tips to make sure you get the most out of your favorite new toy.

Note that, while the features and operations of the iPod, iPod Nano, and iPod Mini are very similar, those of the iPod Shuffle are unique. In spite of this, Shuffle users will find much of the information in Chapter 1 (and the rest of this book) useful and applicable to their iPod experience. They will also find information dedicated to the Shuffle in Chapter 6: Do the Shuffle.

01 Your Battery and You

Once you've got an iPod and you've laid out the contents of your packaging, you'll no doubt want to use it immediately. However, it's wise to develop an awareness for the care and maintenance of your iPod's battery prior to your first charge. To get you off on the right foot, and to ensure a long, satisfying lifespan for your iPod's battery, we'll start with some guidelines and recommendations for battery care.

Rechargeable devices feature a wide array of battery technologies, but there are some fundamental limitations that are almost universally true. In a nutshell, your battery won't last forever, how you use it will affect how long it lasts, and it's most likely a pain and/or expensive to have it replaced.

iPods feature lithium-ion batteries. One of the benefits of lithium-ion batteries is that they can be charged at any time—it isn't necessary to deplete their charge prior to recharging. Lithium-ion batteries also reach approximately 80% of their charge capacity in only an hour or two (in the case of the iPod). An additional two hours allows your iPod's battery to "trickle" charge up to 100%.

A "charge cycle" is consumed every time your iPod uses power equivalent to its battery's full charge capacity. (Note that this isn't dependent on reducing your battery's charge level to zero; several partial charges count as a single charge cycle.) Your battery's maximum charge is reduced by a small amount every time you complete a charge cycle. Apple indicates that your battery should, if properly cared for, retain 80% of its capacity after 400 charge cycles. Some helpful tips for getting the most out of your battery follow.

Keep your iPod up to date. By downloading Apple's software updates you can take advantage of the latest advancements in the software that runs your iPod. These sometimes include improvements to your iPod's battery efficiency. See Apple's support site for software updates: http://www.apple.com/support/ipod/.

Use your iPod regularly. Apple suggests consuming a minimum of one charge cycle per month to keep the juices flowing in your iPod's battery.

Store and operate your iPod at room temperature. Colder and warmer climates adversely affect both the performance and lifespan of your iPod's battery.

The iPod universe is full of recommendations and strategies for minimizing your battery drain. Naturally, the less power you consume, the fewer charge cycles you'll use and the longer your battery will last. A list of general tips follows.

Use the Hold button. Activating your Hold button will prevent your iPod from turning itself on while in storage or transit.

Avoid using the equalizer. Though it may please your ears, the EQ requires additional processing from your iPod. This translates into increased battery consumption. Turn off the equalizer if doing so won't diminish your enjoyment of your iPod. Alter your EQ options through the Settings > EQ menu of your iPod.

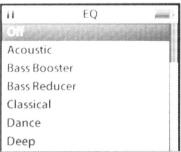

Reduce backlighting. Your iPod allows you to reduce the time that your backlight remains illuminated following button or Click Wheel commands. Reducing your backlight usage saves valuable battery life over time. (You can turn your backlight off completely if you have sufficient ambient lighting.) Change your backlight settings via the Settings > Backlight Timer menu.

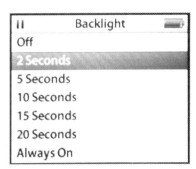

Respect your cache. iPods using hard drives (iPod, iPod Mini) use a memory cache to avoid having to access their drives continually. This saves battery life because the iPod's hard drive consumes a considerable amount of battery power. By using compressed audio—rather than the larger file formats supported by the iPod—you allow the cache to function properly, without having to access the hard drive excessively. You can also facilitate the cache's operation by refraining from skipping tracks. Every time you skip or fast-forward the hard drive must be accessed, and your battery is depleted faster.

Now that we've covered the terrifying ramifications of plugging your iPod in, it's time to do it! Depending on which model you've purchased, your charging hardware will vary. Whether you have a USB or FireWire cable, or a full docking apparatus, consult your iPod's manual to begin the charging procedure.

Note that it is not necessary to charge your iPod for 24 hours on its initial charge; your battery will reach its capacity in three to five hours. (There is no harm in leaving it plugged in once it is fully charged.) Refer to the battery status indicator on your LCD screen for feedback related to your battery's progress.

iPod Nano users should be aware that, although they can charge their iPods using a FireWire cable, they will not be able to transfer files to or from their players via FireWire. Use the USB 2.0 cable included with the Nano for this purpose.

02 Getting to Know Your iPod

Before you can really unlock the power of your iPod, you'll want to familiarize yourself with the device itself. In this technique we'll point out the primary hardware components of your iPod, then introduce some of its basic controls. Note that we'll be covering the iPod, iPod Nano, and iPod Mini here; iPod Shuffle users can turn to Chapter 6 for information specific to the Shuffle.

iPod, iPod Nano, and iPod Mini Hardware

A. **Dock Connector port**: This is the primary data connection for your iPod. A variety of cables and peripherals connect to your iPod through this jack. This is also how your iPod connects to your computer.

B. **Click Wheel**: The Click Wheel allows you to control your iPod. All the menu functions and playback options for your iPod are accessed here. At the top of the Click Wheel is the Menu button, which is used primarily to "back up" to a previous menu when navigating through the iPod's menu system. You'll find the Next/Fast-forward button on the right and the Previous/Rewind button on the left. As their names imply, these are used to navigate through menus and for transport functions. Lastly, the Play/Pause button is located at the bottom of the Click Wheel.

C. **Select button**: Click the Select button to accept the current selection on your iPod's screen.

D. **LCD screen**: This is the display for the iPod operating system. Note that the screen lacks color on Mini models.

E. **Hold button**: Activate the Hold button to lock your iPod in its current state. This prevents your Click Wheel from being manipulated unintentionally.

F. **Headphone/AV port**: In addition to accepting headphones, this port is used to facilitate numerous iPod accessories.

G. **iPod Remote port**: This port comes into play when using a variety of iPod accessories. Note that the iPod Nano lacks a Remote port.

Basic Operations

- To turn on the iPod, press any button.
- To turn off the iPod, press and hold the Play/Pause button for about three seconds.
- To select a menu item, press the Select button.
- To back up to the previous menu, press Menu on the Click Wheel.

Playback Operations

- To browse your audio tracks, select Music from the main menu. Navigate the menu system according to your preferred search method—artist, album, song title, etc.

- Hit the Play button to play the selected track, directory, or playlist. To play all the tracks within a given directory or playlist, highlight the directory or playlist and press the Play button. For example, press the Play button on an artist's name to play all the tracks for that artist.

- Press the Play button while a track is playing to pause play. Press the Play button again to resume play.

- To change the volume, use the Click Wheel while the iPod is on the Now Playing screen. Scrolling clockwise increases the volume; scrolling counterclockwise decreases it.

- When playing multiple tracks, hit the Next/Fast-forward button to skip to the next track. Hit the Previous/Rewind button to return to the beginning of the track. Hit the Previous/Rewind button twice to skip to the previous track.

- To skip to a specific point in the currently playing track, press the Select button at the Now Playing screen. (Notice the change to the progress bar beneath the track information.) Scroll back and forth on the Click Wheel to skip to any point in the track. Remove your thumb from the Click Wheel to resume play at the selected spot.

- You can navigate through your iPod's menus while playing music. When a song is playing, hit the Menu button to initiate menu navigation. If you want to return to the Now Playing screen, hit the Menu button repeatedly until you're at the main menu, then select Now Playing.

- From the main menu, select Shuffle Songs to randomly play the entire contents of your iPod. This will play all the songs on your iPod—except audiobooks and podcasts—in random order.

- Choose Settings > Shuffle to select a shuffle mode for your iPod. With the shuffle option activated, your iPod will enter Shuffle mode by default whenever you press the Play button. Choose the Songs option to shuffle individual tracks within a directory or playlist, or select Albums to shuffle entire albums.

- Select Settings > Repeat to activate Repeat mode. Hit Repeat once to select single-track repeat or twice to repeat all tracks.

- You can also rate the songs on your iPod. While a song is playing, click the Select button three times (twice for Mini users). This brings up the ratings menu for the current track—in the form of five dots. Use the Click Wheel to rate the track from one to five stars. When you've chosen your desired rating, click the Select button to save your rating and return to the Now Playing screen.

Customizing Your iPod Settings

The iPod, iPod Nano, and iPod Mini each offers a variety of options for customizing your settings. Some of these options simply affect your user preferences, while others can dramatically impact your iPod's battery life. In this section, we'll help you tailor your iPod settings to suit your needs.

Select Settings from your iPod's main menu. You'll find the following options:

About: Select the About option to view information related to your iPod's contents. You can view the total number of songs and/or photos on your iPod here as well as the amount of storage space you're currently using. Available storage space is also given. Other information, such as your iPod's firmware version and serial number, is also provided.

II	About	■
	iPod	
Songs		7
Photos		7
Capacity		55.8 GB
Available		55.7 GB
Version		1.2
S/N		

Main Menu: From this menu you can customize what appears on your iPod's main menu screen. Turn options on or off to suit your tastes. We recommend that iPod Nano users use this menu to add the Screen Lock command to their main menus.

Shuffle: With the shuffle option activated, your iPod will enter Shuffle mode by default whenever you press the Play button. Choose the Songs option to shuffle individual tracks within a directory or playlist, or select Albums to shuffle entire albums.

II	Main Menu	■
Music		On
Playlists		Off
Artists		On
Albums		Off
Compilations		On
Songs		Off
Podcasts		Off

Repeat: Use this feature to activate Repeat mode. Press Select once to repeat individual track; press Select again to repeat all the tracks in the currently playing directory or playlist.

Backlight Timer: Select this option to customize your iPod's backlight performance. Choose from a variety of time durations to determine how long your backlight stays on when you touch the controls of your iPod. Alternatively, select Always On to keep your backlight on at all times. Be aware that your backlight usage greatly affects your iPod's battery life (and, in turn, the life span of your battery), so it is recommended that you use it sparingly.

Audiobooks: Select the playback speed for audiobook tracks: Slower, Normal, Faster.

EQ: Select this option to change your sound equalization settings. Apple's preset EQ settings are designed to suit a number of music genres. If you set your iPod's EQ to off, any tracks that have been assigned an EQ preset in iTunes will play on your iPod using their assigned setting. If you set your iPod's EQ to a specific preset, however, this setting will override any track-specific EQ settings. Note that using the EQ will reduce your iPod's battery life.

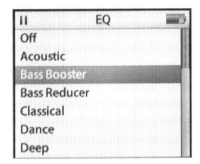

Compilations (iPod and iPod Nano only): iPod and iPod Nano users have the option of grouping together tracks from compilation CDs. When this option is selected, the Compilations folder is added to your iPod's Music menu. Tracks that have been designated as compilation tracks in iTunes appear here, rather than under their individual artist listings. This is useful if you have a number of greatest hits packages in your music collection; by listing these tracks together in the Compilations folder, you avoid littering your Artist folder with hundreds of "one hit wonder" artists.

Sound Check: Your iPod has the same Sound Check feature offered by iTunes. Recorded music is recorded, mastered, and remastered using a wide variety of techniques and technologies. As a result, the volume "embedded" in different audio tracks can vary a great deal. Use Sound Check to keep your iPod's overall volume level the same for all audio tracks. Note that the Sound Check feature must also be activated in iTunes for this to take effect on your iPod. (iTunes must analyze your library to determine how the Sound Check feature treats each track.)

Contrast (iPod Mini only): Use the Contrast control to adjust the contrast of your LCD screen. Generally speaking, you'll want to increase the contrast level as ambient light levels increase.

Clicker: The default setting (Speaker) produces an audible clicking sound that can be heard whenever you manipulate the Click Wheel—even when you aren't listening through headphones. Alternatively, you can route the clicking sound through your headphones or through both your headphones and the speaker. You can also turn the click sound off entirely.

Date & Time: Your iPod syncs its clock to your computer's clock whenever you connect it. However, you do have the option of setting the date and time manually. Choose your time zone, set your time, and choose between 12- and 24-hour time displays. Toggle the Time in Title option to add the time to the title bar at the top of your iPod's display screen. (By default, the title for the current menu is displayed here.)

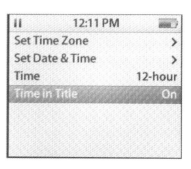

Contacts: Choose sort and display options for your iPod's Contacts menu. (See Technique 17 for more information about your iPod's Contacts feature.)

Language: Change your preferred language for the iPod interface here.

Reset All Settings: Select this option to restore your iPod's settings to their factory defaults. It's a good idea to memorize the location of this menu selection (from the main menu), as it comes in very handy if you accidentally change your iPod's language setting to something you find incomprehensible.

iPod, Meet iTunes

Now that you're familiar with your iPod, it's time to make it do something! The key to everything, of course, is iTunes. In this technique we'll show you how to make your iPod shake hands with iTunes. This is the beginning of a beautiful relationship!

Connecting Your iPod

With your iPod fully charged, connect it to your computer using the included USB 2.0 cable (or aftermarket FireWire cable, if you prefer). The iPod Nano and iPod Mini do not come with a USB Power Adapter, so users of these models will follow the steps given here during their initial battery charge.

iTunes will launch automatically once your iPod is connected. On your first connection with iTunes, you'll be greeted by the iPod Setup Assistant. The assistant will request that you name your iPod and register it with Apple.

You'll also be asked if you want your iPod to automatically sync with iTunes every time it is hooked up to your computer. Options are given both for syncing music and photos (if your iPod supports photos). If you choose to sync your iPod from the setup assistant, your iPod's track library will mirror your iTunes library each time you connect your iPod. (Sync modes are covered in-depth in Techniques 7, 8, and 9.) You can change these settings at any time via iTunes > Preferences > iPod.

When your iPod is connected, an icon representing it appears in the iTunes Source list. Select your iPod from the list to display its contents in the Track and Browser frames.

▲ The iPod Setup Assistant

In the Source list, click the arrow to the left of the iPod icon to reveal any playlists saved to your iPod. Right-click (or Ctrl-click) the iPod icon to open a pop-up menu with additional options. Most importantly, you can access your iPod's preference settings by selecting iPod Options from this menu.

Preferences are divided by category—Music, Podcasts, Photos, Contacts, and Calendars. (Details pertaining to each of these are given in the corresponding sections of this book.)

▲ The iPod's contents are displayed in the Track and Browser frames

▲ The iPod preferences dialog box

Disconnecting Your iPod

It's crucial that you eject your iPod prior to disconnecting it from your computer; failing to do so can create problems with the data stored on your iPod. Several methods for disconnecting your iPod are available.

- Click the small eject icon that appears to the right of your iPod's name in the Source list.
- Select the Eject option from the Controls menu.
- Give the Eject command from the pop-up menu that appears when you right-click (or Ctrl-click) your iPod in the Source list.
- Click the Eject button in the lower-right corner of your iTunes window.
- Eject your iPod from your desktop as you would any other portable storage device. Mac OS X users can simply drag the iPod's icon to the Trash icon in the Dock. Windows users can right-click the iPod icon in their My Computer directory and select Eject from the pop-up menu. Alternatively, PC users can click the Safely Remove Hardware icon in the system tray and select their iPod from the list of devices.

To ensure that your iPod has been properly ejected, refer to its LCD screen. If the display reads, "Do not disconnect," your iPod has not been properly ejected.

Organizing Your Library

Before you share your iTunes library with your iPod, it's important to learn a few things about organizing your music in iTunes. In this section, we'll cover the basics of editing track info, then make some recommendations so that you can maximize the user-friendliness of your library.

Editing Track Info

All of the tracks in your iTunes library are embedded with information tags. These tags—track name, artist, album title, etc.—allow iTunes to organize your library intelligently. They also allow you to search your library or group together tracks using very specific criteria.

Because this information is transferred to your iPod, your iPod's ease of use is largely dependent on the accuracy and sensibility of the track info applied in iTunes. For this reason, we recommend taking the time to do things right where your track info is concerned.

When you import tracks from a CD, iTunes will access the Internet to automatically fill in the most common track tags (unless you disable this feature in your preferences). However, the consistency and accuracy of these tags is usually suspect, so we recommend that you look them over to make sure they work for you.

Beyond what is filled in automatically during the import process, you might choose to add info to your tracks that is meaningful to you (more on this to follow). Keep in mind that your music is organized based entirely on these tags, so it's important to ensure that they make sense to you.

To edit the information for a track in your library, select the desired file in the Track frame, then right-click (or Ctrl-click) and select Get Info from the pop-up menu. Alternatively, choose Get Info from the File menu at the top of the screen. The keyboard shortcut is Command-I (Mac) or Ctrl-I (PC).

Click the Info tab to reveal the track's information. Edit the fields to ensure that everything is accurate, consistent, and to your liking. Click the Next button to accept changes and move to the next track in your library. Click the OK button to accept your changes and close the window. Some helpful tips for organizing your tracks follow:

▲ Select Get Info from the pop up menu to edit the selected track's info.

Solo artist names: For solo artists, names are given in the First, Last format by default. Since both iTunes and the iPod sort artists alphabetically, you may want to manually change the format to Last, First.

Genre: The genres attached to CDs by default are sometimes shockingly misleading. They're also extremely inconsistent; 10 CDs by the same artist might yield 10 different genres in your iTunes library. If you like browsing your music by genre, take the time to label your tracks with genres that mean something to you. If you want to place the latest Metallica CD in the "Polka Rodeo" genre, go for it! Your iPod will gladly play along.

▲ The Get Info dialog box

Year: Often, the year provided by default on a CD reflects its most recent copyright or release date rather than the original release date of the music. You might want to manually update the Year field to reflect when the music is actually from. This will allow you to organize your music by era. (Who wouldn't want a "greatest hits of the '80s" playlist?)

Disc Number: This field may be filled in during CD import. If not, we recommend adding this info yourself. Use it to separate individual discs in multi-CD albums.

Grouping and Comments: These fields can be very useful for adding meaningful keywords to your tracks. These labels come in handy when creating smart playlists (covered in Technique 6). For instance, you might add the word "Live" to the Grouping field of all your live recordings. You can then create a smart playlist that groups together all of the tracks with the "Live" keyword.

▲ Use the Disc Number field to organize multi-CD albums.

Thinking outside the box: Something to keep in mind is that you don't have to use all of the info fields the way you're supposed to; you can get creative if doing so allows you to organize your library in a way that's useful to you. For instance, some people prefer to leave the album title blank for all their music—they simply have no interest in separating or grouping tracks by album. Personally, I dislike that the iTunes and iPod browsers order albums for a single artist alphabetically. I prefer to see my albums listed chronologically. My solution? I simply add the release year to the beginning of all my album titles. This forces iTunes to list them according to my preference.

Editing Track Preferences

Aside from info tags, which are generally recognized by other applications and MP3 players, iTunes offers several Apple-specific options for embedding your listening preferences into your tracks. These preferences are transferred with your tracks to your iPod.

- To rate a track, select the track and right-click (or Ctrl-click), then choose My Rating from the pop-up menu that appears. Choose how many stars you want to give it.

- To attach an Equalizer preset to a song, select the song, right-click (or Ctrl-click), and select Get Info from the pop-up menu. Select the Options tag and use the Equalizer Preset pull-down menu to assign your preferred preset. Note that this setting is transferred to your iPod along with the track; your iPod's EQ must be set to off, however, for the EQ preset to have an effect.

▲ Rating a track

- You can also embed volume adjustments from the Options tab of the Get Info dialog box. This feature is particularly useful for classical and jazz recordings, which often require you to crank up your iPod's volume.

- You may have noticed the Artwork tab in the Get Info window. Use this to attach album artwork to the selected track. If you have an iPod or iPod Nano, this artwork will transfer with your tracks, and you'll be able to view it on your iPod's LCD screen when listening to the track. You can also add artwork by dragging it (either from a Web page or a location on your hard drive) into the Selected Song/Now Playing frame. (A good source for album artwork is http://www.amazon.com.)

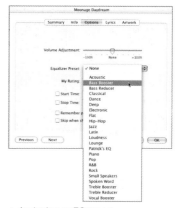

▲ Assigning an EQ preset

Note that adding artwork to a track will increase its file size by the size of the artwork file. Your computer's hard drive can probably handle the load, but you might consider it a waste of space on your iPod—it depends entirely on how cool you think this feature is. Fortunately, you can have it both ways! You can add artwork to your iTunes library, but set iTunes to refrain from transferring this artwork to your iPod. To do this, connect your iPod to your computer, then right-click (or Ctrl-click) your iPod in the Source list and select iPod Options from the pop-up menu. From the Music tab, deselect the "Display album artwork on your iPod" option.

▲ Adding album artwork to a track

06 Creating Playlists in iTunes

Playlists allow you to group your tracks together in ways that are meaningful to you. You might design a playlist for a specific occasion or create one that fits a certain mood. You can even design playlists to last for a certain amount of time or consume a specific amount of hard-drive space. In this section, we'll get you up and running with playlists so that you can maximize the potentials of both iTunes and your iPod.

"Dumb" Playlists

Regular, or "dumb," playlists are the iTunes (and iPod) equivalent of old mix tapes. You build these playlists manually, selecting your songs and their play order by hand.

1. To create a playlist, click the "Create a playlist" button at the lower left of the iTunes window. Alternatively, select New Playlist from the File menu or hit Command-N (Mac) or Ctrl-N (PCs). An untitled playlist will appear in the Source list.

▲ Creating a new playlist

2. To add tracks to your playlist, simply drag them from your library onto the playlist in the Source list.

3. Rename your playlist by clicking it twice (slowly) in the Source list.

▲ Dragging tracks from the Track frame onto the new playlist

4. When your playlist is selected in the Source list, its contents are displayed in the Track frame. Drag and drop songs within your playlist to rearrange their order.

You can create as many playlists as you like. You can also add the same song to multiple playlists without creating duplicates of the original file in your library. (Your playlist is merely a record of your chosen tracks; the tracks themselves are not "stored" there.)

▲ Dragging tracks within a playlist to adjust their play order

To delete a playlist, select it in the Source list and hit the Delete key. Deleting a playlist will not delete its tracks from your library.

Smart Playlists

Smart playlists offer a brilliant method for controlling how you listen to your library—both in iTunes and on your iPod. Smart playlists are playlists that are built automatically using song information. Essentially, you create a smart playlist that describes certain track characteristics. Your smart playlist will dynamically select songs based on your preferences. For instance, you might make a smart playlist that specifies a date range of 1980 to 1989. All the tracks in your library that are from the '80s will be assembled dynamically to create your own personal '80s radio station. Better still, your smart playlist will automatically update itself if you change your iTunes library. In the example given here, if you were to add a CD from 1985 to your library, those tracks would automatically be added to your smart playlist.

To create a smart playlist, follow these steps:

1. Choose New Smart Playlist from the File menu. You can also hold the Option (Mac) or Shift (PC) key and click the "Create a smart playlist" button at the bottom-left corner of the iTunes window.

2. The Smart Playlist dialog box appears. Look over the pull-down menus to get a feel for the criteria you can choose from in building your smart playlist.

3. To add tracks to your playlist that match specific criteria, check the "Match the following rule" option, then make your selection from the pull-down menus. To add additional criteria, click the Add (+) button.

4. To make a smart playlist of a specific size—to match your iPod's storage capacity, perhaps—or length of time, check the "Limit to" option. The pull-down menu provides a variety of ways to limit your playlist.

▲ The Smart Playlist dialog box

5. To include only songs that have a check mark next to them in the iTunes Track frame, select "Match only checked songs."

6. To set iTunes to continually modify your smart playlist as you update and expand your library, make sure "Live updating" is checked.

7. Once you've made your selections, click OK. The smart playlist will be added to your Source list, and its text field will be highlighted to allow you to type in a title. Any songs in your library that match the criteria you set for your smart playlist are added to it automatically.

Smart playlists appear in the Source list with a gear symbol rather than the musical notes used for regular playlists. This allows you to separate different kinds of playlists at a glance.

▲ Note the difference between the smart playlist and regular playlist icons.

lacing Playlists in Folders

With iTunes 5.0, Apple added the ability to group playlists into folders in the iTunes Source list.

1. To create a new playlist folder, select New Folder from the File menu in the iTunes menu bar.

2. When the folder is added to your Source list, its name is highlighted; type in the desired folder name and press the Return key.

3. To create a playlist inside a folder, highlight the folder in the Source list and give the command to create a playlist. The new playlist will automatically appear inside the folder. To create a folder inside a folder, give the New Folder command while the existing folder is highlighted in the Source list.

4. You can click and drag folders and playlists to adjust your organizational structure. As a good place to start, we recommend creating one folder for smart playlists and another folder for regular playlists.

▲ Creating a playlist folder

▲ Organizing playlists using folders and subfolders

NOTE: Although iTunes allows you to organize your playlists using folders, this feature is not supported by any of the iPod models at the time of this writing. Adding a playlist folder to your iPod will simply add the playlists—individually—contained within. A new playlist named after your playlist folder will then be created on your iPod. It will combine all the tracks from the playlists within the folder. With luck, Apple will add true folder support to the iPod with their next software update.

07 Automatic Sync

With properly tagged tracks and a healthy assortment of playlists, it's time to sync your iPod to iTunes. Syncing is the process by which your iTunes library tracks are moved to your iPod. In this section we'll cover the iPod's automatic sync option.

Note that this technique covers syncing procedures for the iPod, iPod Nano, and iPod Mini. Details specific to the Shuffle are covered in Chapter 6: Do the Shuffle.

By default, your iPod is set to automatic sync. This option is pre-checked in the iPod Setup Assistant that pops up the first time you connect your iPod to your computer. Automatic sync, as the name implies, leaves control of your iPod entirely in the hands of iTunes. By selecting this feature, all the library tracks and playlists you've assembled in iTunes will be transferred to your iPod automatically when you connect it to your computer. Updates made to your library or playlists in iTunes will be transferred to your iPod on subsequent syncs.

To initiate automatic sync, simply connect your iPod to your computer. Unless you've changed the sync setting in your iPod's preferences, iTunes will take over from here.

If your iPod has the capacity to hold your entire iTunes library, automatic sync will transfer everything to your player. Your iPod will essentially provide you with a portable copy of your iTunes library. Depending on the number of songs in your library, your initial sync may take quite a length of time. Subsequent syncs will go faster, as only changes made to the library since the last sync will be transferred to your iPod.

If your iPod lacks the capacity to hold your entire library, you'll receive a prompt when you connect it to your computer alerting you to this fact. You'll then be

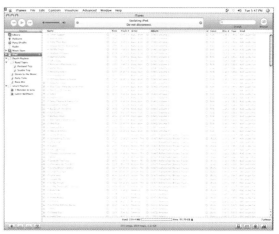

▲ The iTunes window during an automatic iPod update

given the option to create a playlist that represents the portions of your library that will be automatically synced to your iPod. Note that this playlist will be created from tracks randomly selected by iTunes, so we recommend you take control of this process by using the semi-automatic sync method of updating your iPod. (This will be covered in depth in the next technique.)

If you select your iPod from the Source list, its content will appear in the Track frame. The tracks will appear grayed out, and you will not be able to manipulate them in any way.

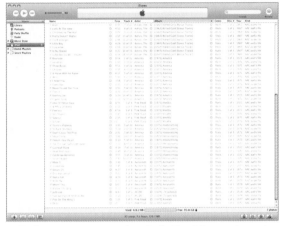

▲ iPod contents are grayed out in the Track frame when using automatic sync.

The iPod icon in the Source list flashes red while your iPod is updating. It's very important that you refrain from disconnecting your iPod from your computer prior to completion of the update process. The track info display at the top of the iTunes window will alert you when the update process is complete.

If, while your iPod is connected, you make changes to your library that you would like to transfer to your iPod immediately, you must manually initiate an update. Do this by right-clicking (or Ctrl-clicking) your iPod's icon in the Source list and selecting Update from the pop-up menu. Alternatively, you can select your iPod from the Source list and choose the Update option from the File menu.

iPod update is complete.

▲ The track info display will alert you when the update is complete.

▲ Initiating an automatic update manually

08 Semi-Automatic Sync

Under certain conditions you'll want to limit the degree to which your iPod library matches your iTunes library. The most obvious of these scenarios is if your iTunes library is larger than the capacity of your iPod. For this technique, we'll cover semi-automatic syncing, which allows you to specify which parts of your library are transferred to your iPod during automatic updates.

Note that this technique covers syncing procedures for the iPod, iPod Nano, and iPod Mini. Details specific to the Shuffle are covered in Chapter 6: Do the Shuffle.

To explore your iPod's semi-automatic sync options, connect your iPod to your computer, wait for iTunes to launch, and open the iPod preferences dialog box. From the Music tab, check the "Automatically update selected playlists only" option. All of your playlists appear in the list beneath this option. Simply place a check next to the playlists you wish to update when you connect your iPod to your computer. Click OK to accept your changes and close the preferences dialog box.

The most obvious use for semi-automatic sync is if your iTunes library is larger than the capacity of your iPod. Simply create a playlist and drag your favorite on-the-go music into it. With your playlist selected in the Source list, pay close attention to its size—displayed at the bottom of the iTunes window. You'll want to keep this below the storage capacity of your iPod.

Alternatively, you can get creative using smart playlists. Smart playlists can be limited to a specific total file size; simply set the limit to the capacity of your iPod, and your playlist will never run long. (See Technique 6 for an introduction to smart playlists.)

▲ Setting up semi-automatic sync

44 songs, 1.8 hours, 111.9 MB

▲ The total size for the currently selected playlist is displayed at the bottom of the iTunes window.

For example, if you have a 4 GB iPod Nano that cannot hold your entire iTunes library, you might create a smart playlist that includes 3 GB of music from the jazz genre that you have not listened to in iTunes in the last month. You might then create a playlist that adds 1 GB of music recorded between 1990 and 1999 for a "hits of the '90s" package. Enter your iPod preferences, select both playlists for syncing, and you're good to go.

▲ Creating a smart playlist that includes a size limit

Your imagination is the only limit when creating playlists for semi-automatic syncing. Here are some suggestions:

- If you've rated your tracks in iTunes, make a smart playlist of all your top-rated songs.

- If you've taken the time to add beats-per-minute info to your tracks, create a playlist using only songs that match the tempo of your workout routine.

- If you take a lot of road trips, make a manual playlist with your best road music—just make sure "Born to Be Wild" is there.

- Create a smart playlist using "Abba" as the defining criteria, name it "Absurd Swedish Disco," and impress your coworkers at the next all-employee meeting!

09

Transferring Audio Manually

There is a third option for delivering audio to your iPod; you can manage the contents of your iPod manually, dragging and dropping tracks, directories, and playlists by hand. Go that manual route if you simply prefer to do everything yourself.

Note that this technique covers manual operations for the iPod, iPod Nano, and iPod Mini. Details specific to the Shuffle are covered in Chapter 6: Do the Shuffle.

To manage the contents of your iPod manually, connect your iPod and bring up the iPod preferences dialog box. Check the "Manually manage songs and playlists" option, then click OK to close the preferences window.

Once manual operation is selected, the iPod icon in your Source list comes alive. Select it to reveal the contents of your iPod in the Track frame. Notice that the tracks are no longer grayed out; you can select them and manipulate them as you would tracks in your iTunes library. You can even delete them from your iPod.

Drag and drop tracks from your library onto the iPod icon in the Source list to transfer them to your iPod. Do the same to transfer playlists or directories. Click the arrow icon to the left of your iPod's icon to reveal the playlists currently on your iPod. You can alter or delete these without

▲ Setting the iPod for manual operation

changing their counterparts in your iTunes library. You can also create playlists directly on your iPod; simply select your iPod from the Source list and create a playlist as you normally would—the new playlist will appear directly on your iPod. Note that if a song is already on your iPod and you drag it from your iTunes library to one of your iPod's playlists, the original track will not be duplicated; your iPod "knows" to merely add the track to the playlist without transferring the song over again.

One of the primary benefits of manual operation is that you don't have to worry about how your changes in iTunes might impact your iPod. For instance, you can delete tracks from iTunes without losing those tracks on your iPod the next time you connect it to your computer.

The principal drawback of manual operation is that your iPod will not communicate track data back to iTunes upon syncing. When using automatic or semi-automatic sync, song ratings and play-count statistics (i.e., how many times you've played each track) are transferred from your iPod to iTunes during updates. This is not the case when working in manual mode. Of course, whether this matters to you depends entirely on how you use your iPod.

▲ Managing the iPod's contents manually using the Track frame

Note that controlling your iPod's music manually, does not preclude syncing other data automatically; you can still update photos, contacts, and calendar events automatically. See Chapter 3 for additional details.

📀 Power User's Tip

If you choose to operate your iPod manually, you can listen to music on your iPod through the iTunes interface. While the music files on your iPod can't be copied to another iTunes library due to rights restrictions, this option does come in handy if you want to play a friend's iPod through your computer's speaker system (or vice versa). In other words, it's great at parties!

On-the-Go Playlists

Playlists offer a handy method for creating track sequences that suit your tastes. But you don't need iTunes to take advantage of playlists on your iPod. In this section, we'll introduce on-the-go playlists, which you can create directly on your iPod.

Creating and Saving On-the-Go Playlists

To create an on-the-go playlist, do the following:

1. From your iPod's main menu, select Music and browse to the playlist, directory, or track you wish to add to your on-the-go playlist.

2. Highlight your selection, then press and hold the Select button until your selection flashes. The tracks have been added to your on-the-go playlist.

3. Repeat the previous step with any other selections you wish to add to your on-the-go playlist. Each additional selection will be added to the playlist.

4. Select On-The-Go from your Playlist menu to access your on-the-go playlist.

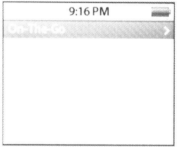

▲ Access your on-the-go playlist from the Playlist menu

To play the entire on-the-go playlist, press the Play button with the On-The-Go option highlighted in your Playlist menu. Alternatively, click the Select button to navigate to specific tracks in your playlist. To remove a song from your on-the-go playlist, highlight the song in the playlist and hold the Select button until the song title flashes. To clear the contents of the on-the-go playlist, select Clear Playlist from the On-The-Go menu (this option appears beneath the tracks in the playlist).

▲ Clearing the on-the-go playlist

You also have the option of saving the current on-the-go playlist so that you can create a new one. To do this, select Save Playlist from the On-The-Go menu (you'll find this option at the bottom of the menu). The current on-the-go playlist is saved as "New Playlist 1" in the Playlists menu. Subsequent on-the-go playlists are saved using sequential numbers.

▲ On-the-go playlists are saved using a sequential numbering scheme.

ⓣransferring On-the-Go Playlists to iTunes

What happens to your saved playlists the next time you connect your iPod to your computer depends entirely on your sync method of choice. Here's a quick breakdown of how things work:

Automatic sync: iTunes will import on-the-go playlists from your iPod to the iTunes Source list, naming them On-The-Go 1, On-The-Go 2, etc. If you rename the iTunes versions of these playlists, their names will be updated on your iPod the next time you connect it to your computer.

Semi-automatic sync: Again, iTunes will copy your on-the-go playlists to the iTunes Source list. However, at the same time these playlists will be deleted from your iPod. Why? Because you've specified in iTunes that only certain playlists should sync to your iPod; because they were created on your iPod, your new on-the-go playlists can't possibly be set to sync automatically. To correct this, allow iTunes to copy your on-the-go playlists to the Source list, then open your iPod preferences and add these playlists to your list of synced playlists (by placing a check next to their names). These playlists will be transferred back to your iPod the next time you connect it to your computer.

Manual: If you're managing your iPod manually, your on-the-go playlists will not be copied to iTunes automatically. Drag and drop these playlists from your iPod to your Source list to copy them into iTunes.

Transcoding Audio

Transcoding is the process of converting an audio file from one format to another. This becomes very important if you import your CD collection using Apple's lossless audio format as your resulting iTunes library may be too large for your iPod. If this is the case, you'll need to convert your tracks into a lossy format prior to transferring them to your iPod. For Technique 11, we'll describe our preferred method for transcoding a library.

Unfortunately, iTunes does not currently support transcoding, so it is necessary to jump through a hoop or two to accomplish this. We warn you in advance that the process described here is a bit of a pain, but the rewards—maintaining a lossless iTunes library—are worth the effort. At least, they are in this author's opinion!

WARNING: Transcoding from one lossy format to another lossy format is not recommended. Each time a lossy conversion is applied to a track, the sound quality of that track is reduced. It's recommended that you only use the following transcoding technique if you've created your library using the Apple Lossless format.

With your AL library properly imported and tagged, complete the following steps to transcode to a lossy format (in this case, Apple's AAC format):

1. Start by changing your import settings to reflect the format you'll be transcoding your lossless library into. In this case, we've chosen the AAC format with the High Quality preset.

▲ Changing the import settings

2. Select the tracks you wish to transcode in the iTunes Track frame. Even if your iPod lacks the capacity to hold your entire transcoded library, you should convert all of your tracks if your computer's available hard-drive space permits. By doing so you'll maximize your options when it comes to transferring tracks to your iPod later. With the desired tracks highlighted, right-click (or Ctrl-click) and select the "Convert selection to" option from the pop-up menu. Alternatively, select this option from the Advanced menu in the iTunes menu bar.

▲ Giving the command to transcode tracks

3. iTunes will convert the selected tracks to your chosen lossy format. This may take quite a while, depending on the import settings you've chosen, the processing power of your computer, and the number of tracks in your library. Notice the Converting Songs listing that appears in the Source list. Select this to review the progress of your conversion on a track-by-track basis.

4. When the conversion process is over, you'll notice that you have duplicate listings for every track in your library. In short, you have a mess on your hands. Don't panic! Select New Smart Playlist from the File menu. Under "Match the following conditions," select Kind from the first pull-down menu, select Contains from the second pull-down menu, and type "AAC" in the text field. Click OK and name your new smart playlist "AAC Library". Create another smart playlist. Set it up as you did the last one, but enter "Apple Lossless" in the text field. Click OK and name this playlist "AL Library."

▲ Creating a smart playlist to separate AAC tracks from AL tracks

5. Select either AAC Library or AL Library from the Source list. If you have the Kind column displayed in your Track frame, you'll notice that the smart playlists you've created automatically separate your AL tracks from your AAC tracks. If you select Library from the Source list you will still see mixed tracks, but you can simply use your AL Library playlist to browse and play music on your computer from now on. Select Show Browser from the Edit menu to display the browser while viewing your smart playlists.

▲ Using smart playlists to isolate each version of the library

6. We'll now configure your semi-automatic sync settings so that your iPod only syncs to your AAC library. Connect your iPod to your computer and bring up the iPod preferences dialog box. (If your iPod starts to update automatically, click the "x" icon to the right of the track info display to cancel the update.) Chose to update only the selected playlists, then place a check next to the AAC Library listing. Click OK to close the preferences window. On subsequent syncs your iPod will ignore your massive AL library and sync only to your AAC library.

To add additional music to your iTunes library (and, in turn, your iPod), remember to change your import preferences back to Apple Lossless prior to importing new CDs. Change your import settings back to AAC prior to transcoding new tracks to AAC.

▲ Syncing only the AAC library

Note that if you want to sync other playlists to your iPod, you must ensure they include only AAC tracks. When creating playlists manually, only drag tracks from your AAC Library playlist. When creating smart playlists, add the same Kind criteria that you used to create your AAC Library playlist (see step 4).

Granted, this is all a bit of pain, and the hassle involved is not for everyone. But until Apple adds this functionality to iTunes, this trick is your best option for importing CDs in a lossless format without sacrificing the song capacity of your iPod.

40 iPod Techniques

Expanding Your Audio Collection

Now that you're familiar with the basic operations of your iPod, it's time to explore some of your options for expanding your iTunes library—beyond the traditional route of importing CDs.

In Chapter 2 we'll introduce you to the iTunes Music Store (iTMS), where you can purchase an enormous range of audio files for use on your iPod. We'll also tell you about audiobooks, which are considerably more convenient (and less expensive) on your iPod than they are on CD. We'll wrap up by discussing podcasts and sources of free music—lawful free music, that is.

12 Exploring the iTunes Music Store

The iTunes Music Store (iTMS) offers an extraordinary array of audio that you can pay for and download directly through iTunes. Naturally, the next stop for these tracks is your iPod. In this section we'll discuss the basic operations of the iTMS and tell you how to get the music found there onto your iPod.

Navigating the iTMS

To begin, you'll need an Internet connection to access the iTMS. With a connection in place, open iTunes and click on the Music Store icon in the Source list. After briefly accessing the Web, the iTunes Track frame will change into the iTMS home page. In addition to various methods for navigating the store, the home page features music-and Apple-related news. You'll also find links to new releases, iTMS exclusives, and staff favorites.

From the "Inside the Music Store" navigation area—found at the upper left of the iTMS window—you can navigate to the main areas of the store. When you leave the storefront a navigational bar appears at the top of the iTMS window; you'll find back, forward, and home buttons here, as well as buttons that assist your browsing—genre, artist, and album.

▲ The iTMS storefront

Search the store using the Search Music Store field found in the upper-right corner of the iTunes window. After entering a keyword and hitting the Return key, your results are displayed in the main iTMS window. You can narrow these results using the Search Bar, which appears at the top of the iTMS window.

Every track in the store features a 30-second sample recording. Simply highlight the track and press play in iTunes to hear the sample. You can even drag and drop previews into your iTunes library (or individual playlists) so that you can listen to them later without having to track them down at the iTMS.

▲ Narrowing search results using the Search Bar

At the time of this writing, all songs at the iTMS are priced at $0.99. Albums usually cost between $10 and $12. Click the Add/Buy Song button to purchase an individual track or the Add/Buy Album button to purchase an entire album. (The button you see depends on your iTunes preferences.) Tracks are encoded at a bit rate of 128 kbps in the AAC format, and all tracks include their corresponding album cover artwork.

Creating an Account

Before you purchase music at the iTMS you'll need to register your account information with the site. To create an iTMS account, click on the Account button at the upper right of the iTMS window. You will get a prompt asking you to log in using your Apple ID or AOL login info. If you don't have an existing account, click on Create New Account.

▲ The iTMS account sign-in dialog box

If you are creating an account, a terms-of-service notice will appear. Click "Agree" and you'll be taken through the account setup process. Once you set up your account, you have the option of purchasing music with a single mouse click or through a shopping-cart system. You can choose between these options from the Store tab of your iTunes preferences. If you go with the shopping cart option, you can view the tracks in your cart by clicking the Shopping Cart option in the iTunes Source list (directly beneath the Music Store listing).

▲ Choosing the shopping cart option from the iTunes preferences window

Digital Rights Management (DRM)

Tracks purchased through the iTMS are embedded with DRM technology. The rules and limitations for these tracks follow:

1. You can burn your tracks to disc an unlimited number of times. However, if your purchased tracks are on a playlist that you're burning to disc, you will need to alter the playlist after burning seven CDs from it.

2. You can listen to your music on an unlimited number of iPods.

3. You can store and listen to your music on five computers.

To play tracks on your computer, you must "authorize" your computer to play them. To authorize or deauthorize your computer, select your desired option from the Advanced menu and follow the prompts to complete the process.

▲ Deauthorizing a computer from the Advanced menu

13 Heard Any Good Books Lately?

Audiobooks, traditionally distributed on cassette and CD, have made a big splash in the digital realm. With thousands of titles to choose from, they offer a great way to maximize your enjoyment of your iPod.

Purchasing Audiobooks from the iTMS

Purchasing audiobooks on the Web offers two massive advantages over buying books on CD: you won't have to import CDs prior to transferring files to your iPod, and you'll almost certainly pay a lot less.

For iPod users, the easiest (and probably the best) place to purchase audiobooks is the iTMS, of course. Select Music Store from your iTunes Source list and click the Audiobooks link at the upper left of the iTMS home page.

▲ The audiobook home page

From the audiobook home page, select a category from the list on the left to browse titles. Alternatively, enter keywords in the Search Music Store field—found at the upper right of the iTMS window—to locate a specific author or book. Click on an author's name at any time to view all of the titles available by that author. Purchase and preview books as you would music tracks.

You'll notice that audiobooks at the iTMS are significantly less expensive than their "real world" counterparts. Because audiobooks purchased through the iTMS lack packaging and don't require shipping of any kind, you aren't charged the corresponding markups. Audiobooks start at around $3.

▲ An author's home page at the iTMS

Purchasing Audiobooks from Audible.com

There are other audiobook stores online. The largest of these (and the most directly supported by your iPod) is Audible.com (http://www. audible.com). Much of Audible's content is available through the iTMS, but their Web site offers a more audiobook-centric atmosphere and a wider selection of titles. Also, the iTMS can be frustrating at times when you're searching for titles (its search features are clearly geared toward music), so Audible.com might yield results with a bit less frustration.

Audible also offers monthly memberships for frequent "readers." With their basic package, you pay a monthly fee to access one audiobook and one periodical (or radio program) per month. For a higher price, you can access two audiobooks per month. Members also receive discounts on audiobook purchases.

▲ The Audible.com home page

Enjoying Audiobooks on Your iPod

No matter how you acquire audiobook files, your end goal is clear: listening to your favorite titles on your iPod. To do this you must first add your audiobook files to your iTunes library. If you've purchased tracks through the iTMS, they'll appear in your iTunes library automatically. If you've purchased them through another provider, simply drag and drop the files into iTunes to add them to your library. Finally, if you've purchased books on CD, import the tracks as you would any music CD. Once your audiobook files are part of your iTunes library, you're only a sync away from "reading" books on your iPod!

To adjust the playback speed of audiobooks on your iPod, select Settings > Audiobooks from your iPod's main menu. Your choices are Slower, Normal, and Faster.

Your iPod and iTunes will "talk to each other" when syncing audiobook files. If you listen to audiobook tracks in either environment, your place will be saved and transferred when you sync your iPod. For example, if you listen to a book on your iPod, then sync your iPod to iTunes, you'll pick up in the spot you left off the next time you listen to that book in iTunes.

14 Podcasts

Podcasts offer an exciting new frontier for using your iPod. At the very least, they ensure that you'll never—and we do mean never—run out of things to listen to on your iPod. The best thing is, of course, they're free (at least for now)! In this section we'll introduce you to the bold new world of podcasts.

What's a Podcast, and How Do I Get One?

You might have heard the hubbub surrounding podcasts. High hopes are placed on their role in the future of information and media. What are they? Podcasts are essentially subscription-based audio programs. Newscasts, magazine reports, blog transmissions, television shows—you name it and there's probably a podcast of it. You might say that podcasts are the ultimate marriage of radio and the World Wide Web. Essentially, they're radio that you can take anywhere and listen to any time you want.

Though podcasts are in their infancy, there is already a staggering array of options. If you have a favorite radio program, you can almost certainly find recordings of it in podcast form (don't worry if it isn't a local station). Interested in a missed news report? You're probably covered. If you're a sports fan, prepare to go nuts.

As you might expect by now, for iPod users, the easiest place to find podcasts is the iTMS. Start by clicking the Podcast icon in the iTunes Source list. (Note that you will need at least version 4.9 of iTunes to access this feature.) Your podcast directory will be blank at first, but as you subscribe to podcasts they will appear in this frame. You will also download and manage your podcast subscriptions from this location.

If you click the Settings button at the bottom right of the iTunes window, you'll be taken to the Podcasts tab of your iTunes preferences. Here you can set the frequency with which iTunes checks for new podcasts, determine the method for downloading new podcasts, and set parameters that determine how long podcasts remain in your iTunes library.

▲ Podcast preferences

With Podcasts selected in the Source list, click the Podcast Directory button at the bottom of the Track frame. This takes you directly to the podcast home page of the iTMS. From here you can find an unbelievable array of podcasts to choose from. From professional/commercial/corporate all the way down to "some guy sitting in his basement," the full spectrum of the podcast universe is laid out for your perusal. There are thousands of podcasts available, and that number is growing at an incredible rate. I hope you bought that 60 GB iPod!

▲ The Podcast home page at the iTMS

When browsing the iTMS for podcasts, click on a podcast to be taken to a screen that provides information on the podcast, as well as options for listening to or downloading episodes. You can also subscribe to the podcast by clicking the Subscribe button.

If you only want to download a particular episode, click the Get Episode button and you'll be taken back to your iTunes podcast directory where the podcast will start downloading. Note that some podcasts only offer downloads if you've subscribed to the podcast. You can unsubscribe at any time, so there's little harm in jumping through this hoop to acquire an episode that interests you.

▲ A podcast info page

To listen to an episode in iTunes, play it as you would any music track (once it's finished downloading, of course). A blue dot will appear to the left of any podcast if you haven't listened to that episode yet.

To subscribe to a podcast that you've downloaded an episode from, click the Subscribe button next to the podcast's title in the podcast directory. When you subscribe to a podcast, all the available episodes appear in your directory. Episodes that you haven't downloaded are grayed out. To download these episodes, click the Get button that appears to the right of their titles. To delete an episode, select the episode and hit the Delete key on your keyboard.

▲ The podcast directory

At the bottom right of the iTunes window you'll find the Unsubscribe button. Select a podcast for which you'd like to cancel your subscription and click this button. You'll no longer receive new episodes. Note that hitting the Unsubscribe button will not delete the episodes you already have.

To completely remove a podcast from your library, select the podcast's folder in your podcast directory and hit the Delete key on your keyboard. You will unsubscribe from the podcast, and all its episodes will be removed from your library.

Naturally, there are other venues on the Web for finding and downloading podcasts. Some good sites to get you started follow:

http://www.podcastalley.com
http://www.podcast.net
http://www.indiepodder.org

Podcasts on Your iPod

The potential of podcasts really comes into focus when you think about listening to them on your iPod. Like listening to the news during your morning commute, but your local radio options are pathetic? Choose from countless podcasts, transfer them to your iPod, and you're good to go. You can even pause and resume play if that smelly guy next to you on the bus won't stop mumbling to his invisible friend. (Why doesn't he realize it's an argument he can't win?)

Or perhaps you've got a road trip coming up and you're fairly certain the radio programming out in cow territory isn't up to snuff. Again, load your iPod with podcasts suited to your tastes, and you'll never veer into a ditch again.

Transferring Podcasts to Your iPod

Of course, before you can do any of that, you'll need to move your podcasts to your iPod. With your iPod connected, bring up your iPod preferences and select the Podcasts tab. From here you can set your sync preferences just as you would for music. Use the automatic sync option to reproduce your iTunes podcast library on your iPod each time you sync. Use the semi-automatic option to update only select podcasts. Lastly, select the "Do not update Podcasts" option to handle everything manually. Use the Update pull-down menu to specify which episodes are updated on your iPod.

▲ The Podcasts tab of the iPod preferences window

Podcasts can also be added to iTunes playlists. Drag and drop episodes to add them to manual playlists, or create smart playlists to sort podcasts based on your selected criteria.

Listening to Podcasts on Your iPod

If your iPod's software is up to date, a Podcasts option will appear in its Music menu. If your iPod lacks this feature, see Technique 39 for instructions for updating your software. Select Podcasts from the Music menu to display the podcasts on your iPod. Select one of the podcasts to see the list of episodes available for that podcast. Play episodes as you would music tracks.

Note that, as with audiobooks, your iPod will transfer your place in an episode to iTunes when syncing (and vice versa).

15 Free Music, the Lawful Way

Though they aren't always easy to find, there are free tunes waiting for you out on the Web. We're talking legitimately free tunes—the kind that won't get you slapped with a lawsuit. In this section, we'll cover a few options for tracking down free music.

The easiest way to get free music is right at the iTMS. Apple runs a promotional event called New Music Tuesdays; every Tuesday the iTMS offers one free (pre-selected) download. Simply head to the iTMS once a week to see if you're interested in the current offering. You might want to set your iPod to alert you of this each Tuesday so you don't miss any opportunities (see Technique 18 for the scoop on your iPod's calendar feature).

▲ The iTMS single of the week

Amazon.com also offers free music downloads. Head to http://www.amazon.com, go to the Music area of the site, and look for the "Free Downloads" link at the top of your browser window. Amazon doesn't restrict their free downloads to a single track, so you can browse numerous listings to find something that interests you.

NPR.org also offers free music. Another good resource for finding free music (or almost anything else related to the iPod) is http://ilounge.com. You'll find multiple links to free download sites here; simply click the Free Music link at the top of the site.

▲ Amazon's Free Music Downloads page

Perhaps the best sources of free tracks are the Web sites for individual artists that litter the Web. Artists often promote their CD releases through their own sites, and these promotions sometimes include free sample tracks from upcoming albums. Track down the official sites for each of your favorite artists, and bookmark them in your Web browser. Check in periodically to see if there are any goodies available for free.

As a final word, it's important to be careful when tracking down music on the Web. Free music sites must demonstrate they have the legal authority to distribute the music they're offering for download. Even sites that require payment for tracks aren't "legit" simply because you're paying to access their files. Your best defense against illegally downloading music is a healthy amount of suspicion; if a site seems shady, it probably is.

40 iPod Techniques

Beyond Audio—iPod Extras

Though the iPod is first and foremost a music player, it offers several additional features that bring basic PDA functionality to the table for iPod, iPod Nano, and iPod Mini users. (Sorry, Shufflers!) In this chapter we'll explore your iPod's "extras."

We'll close out the chapter with a discussion of third-party software. By using programs beyond Apple's offerings you just might unlock the hidden potential of your iPod....

16 Clocks

Your iPod offers a clock as well as sleep and alarm functions. In this section, we'll get you up and running with each of these features.

Clock—iPod and iPod Mini

Select Extras > Clock to view the time on your iPod. Note that, at the time of this writing, the clock featured on the iPod and iPod Mini is different than the one offered by the iPod Nano. (This may change in a future software update, however.)

Your iPod will automatically sync to your computer's clock when you connect it to your system. In fact, you can live a long life with your iPod without ever having to set its clock manually. If, however, you do need to set your iPod's clock manually for any reason, follow these steps:

1. Select Extras > Clock > Date & Time > Set Date & Time from the main menu to manually set the time. Alternatively, navigate to Settings > Date & Time.

2. Use the Click Wheel to cycle through numbers and use the Next/Fast-forward and Previous/Rewind buttons to move through the different number fields. (You can also hit the Select button to proceed to the next number field.) After entering the year, press the Select or Next/Fast-forward button to set the time and return to the Date & Time menu.

3. At the Date & Time menu choose between 12- and 24-hour time displays. You can also determine whether the time appears in the title bar of your iPod's display. Lastly, you can select your time zone—particularly useful if you travel a lot, as you won't have to manually set the time if you change time zones. iPod Nano users, of course, have a better option for dealing with this....

Clock—iPod Nano

Apple has upgraded the iPod's clock feature for iPod Nano users. (Let's hope those of us with iPods or iPod Minis get a software upgrade for our clocks soon!) iPod Nano users can save multiple world-time clocks, setting unique preferences for each saved clock. Needless to say, this is a wonderful feature if you travel a lot. To use your iPod Nano's clock, do the following:

1. Note that iPod Nano users cannot set their date and time within the Extras > Clock directory. They must access this from the Settings > Date & Time menu. From there, follow the steps given previously (for the iPod and iPod Mini) to set your primary clock.

2. Navigate to Extras > Clock from the main menu. Your saved world clocks are listed here.

3. To add a new clock, scroll to the bottom of your clock list and select the New Clock option. Select a world region, then a city within that region. A clock for that city will be added to your clock menu.

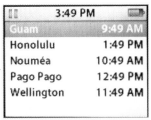

4. To enter the submenu of any clock in your list, highlight it using the Click Wheel and press the Select button. From here you can access alarm functions, change the city associated with the clock, toggle daylight savings time, delete the clock entirely from your Clock menu, or set the sleep timer.

Alarm Clock

The iPod, iPod Nano, and iPod Mini all have an alarm clock function built in.

1. iPod and iPod Mini users can access the alarm clock from the main menu by selecting Extras > Clock > Alarm Clock. iPod Nano users must select a specific clock from the Clock menu prior to setting an alarm.

2. Set the Alarm option to On, then proceed to the Time submenu to set the time for your alarm.

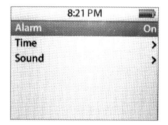

3. Navigate to the Sound submenu to choose a sound for your alarm. If you select Beep, the alarm will sound through the iPod's internal speaker. (Unless you are an extremely light sleeper, this option won't be useful for waking you up.) If you select a song or playlist, you will need to have your iPod connected to external speakers or headphones. If you prefer a traditional alarm sound, you might want to load one onto your iPod as an audio file, create an on-the-go playlist from it, then select that playlist as your alarm sound. Just keep in mind that your iPod can't wake you up if its battery dies—make sure it's properly charged before you hit the hay.

Sleep Timer

The Sleep Timer option (accessible from the Clock menu for iPod and iPod Mini users, and from any saved clock's menu for iPod Nano users) turns off your iPod after playing music for a predetermined time. If your iPod supports photos, you have the option of using the sleep timer with photo slideshows as well.

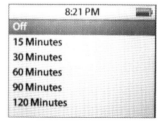

Contacts

One of the best extras offered by the iPod is its ability to store contacts. Though your iPod can't send emails or make phone calls (yet!), it can store countless email addresses and phone numbers. In this section we'll show you how to get the most from your iPod's contacts feature.

To begin, it's important to note that Mac users and Windows users will have different experiences when using the iPod's contacts feature. Why? Because Apple makes a suite of programs (Address Book, iCal, and iPhoto) that work seamlessly with iPods connected to Macs. Sadly, these programs are not available to Windows users. However, though their paths may be different, users of iPods on both platforms will get to the same destination: an iPod stuffed with contact info.

Adding Contacts to Your iPod—Mac Users

Connect your iPod to your computer, open iTunes, and bring up the iPod preferences dialog box. Select the Contacts tab and check the "Synchronize Address Book contacts" option. You can sync all your contacts or only selected groups.

▲ The Contacts tab of the iPod preferences window

If you use a third-party program (rather than Apple's Address Book) to store contact information on your computer, you can still import contacts to your iPod—it simply isn't automated. Start by enabling your iPod for disk usage (from the Music tab of your iPod preferences). Your iPod should now appear on your desktop.

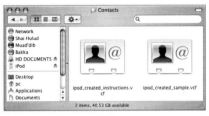

▲ The iPod's Contacts folder

You can now transfer contact files directly to your iPod's Contacts folder. However, the iPod can only recognize files in a specific format: vCard (.vfc). Many popular programs—Palm Desktop, Microsoft Outlook, Microsoft Entourage, and Eudora—are capable of exporting contacts in this format. See your program's documentation for instructions.

With your contacts exported in the proper format, drag and drop them into your iPod's Contacts folder, eject your iPod from your computer, and you're good to go.

Adding Contacts to Your iPod—Windows Users

Connect your iPod to your computer, open iTunes, and bring up the iPod preferences dialog box. Select the Contacts tab and check the "Synchronize contacts from [Outlook/Outlook Express]" option. You can sync all your contacts or only selected groups.

As with the Mac, you have the option of importing contacts from programs other than Outlook and Outlook Express, but the process isn't automated. Start by enabling your iPod for disk usage (from the Music tab of the iPod preferences dialog box). Your iPod should now appear as a drive in your My Computer directory.

You can now transfer contact files directly to your iPod's Contacts folder. However, the iPod can only recognize files in a specific format: vCard (.vfc). Many popular programs are capable of exporting contacts in this format. See your program's documentation for instructions.

▲ The Contacts tab of the iPod preferences dialog box—Windows version

With your contacts exported in the vCard format, drag and drop them in your iPod's Contacts folder, eject your iPod from your computer, and you're good to go.

Workarounds

All is not lost if your third-party contacts program does not export in the vCard format. Many programs allow you to export contacts in some format. These files can, in turn, often be imported into programs that do support the vCard format (Address Book and Outlook among them). It can be a bit tricky (depending on which program you're using and which options it gives you for exporting your data) and there's a definite hassle to it, but at least it's possible! Consult your software's documentation for instructions.

Viewing Contacts on Your iPod

Select Extras > Contacts from the main menu, and your contacts are listed for your perusal. Choose Settings > Contacts from the main menu to change how your contacts are sorted and displayed in the Contacts menu; you can choose between "Last, First" and "First, Last" naming conventions.

NOTE: You cannot edit contact information (or enter new contacts) on your iPod. Unfortunately, the iPod's contact feature is a one-way street at this stage in the device's evolution.

18 Calendars

Bringing additional PDA features to the table, your iPod has a surprisingly impressive calendar feature. In this technique, we'll walk you through the basics.

As with contacts, Mac and Windows users will have different experiences using the iPod's calendar feature. Just as Apple's Address Book syncs contacts for Mac users, their iCal program syncs calendar events. Fortunately, though they can't use iCal, Windows users aren't left out in the cold.

Adding Calendar Events to Your iPod—Mac Users

Connect your iPod to your computer, open iTunes, and bring up the iPod preferences dialog box. Select the Calendars tab and check the "Synchronize iCal calendars" option. You can either sync all your calendars or selected calendars. Note that your iPod will import to-do lists from iCal in addition to calendar events.

If you use a program other than iCal to store calendar events on your Mac, you can transfer these events to your iPod manually. Start by enabling your iPod for disk usage (from the Music tab of the iPod preferences dialog box). Your iPod should now appear on your desktop.

▲ The Calendars tab of the iPod preferences window

You can now transfer calendar files directly to your iPod's Calendars folder. However, just as manually transferred contacts must be saved in a specific file format, so must your calendar events—in this case, the iCal (.ics) file format. See your program's documentation for instructions for exporting in this format (if your program supports the iCal format). With your calendar events exported in the proper format, drag and drop them into your iPod's Calendars folder, eject your iPod, and you're all set.

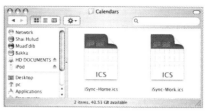

▲ The iPod's Calendars folder

Adding Calendar Events to Your iPod—Windows Users

Connect your iPod to your computer, open iTunes, and bring up the iPod preferences dialog box. Select the Calendars tab and select your sync options for Microsoft Outlook.

As with the Mac, you can transfer calendar events from other programs, but the process isn't automated. First, enable your iPod for disk usage (from the Music tab of the iPod preferences dialog box). Your iPod should now appear as a drive in your My Computer folder.

You can now transfer calendar event files directly to your iPod's Calendars folder. These events, however, must be saved in the iCal (.ics) file format. Several popular calendar programs export events in this format. See your program's documentation for instructions.

With your calendar events exported in the iCal format, drag and drop them into your iPod's Calendars folder, eject your iPod, and you're ready to go.

Note that Windows users cannot access the to-do list functionality of their iPods; this feature is only enabled for Mac users using the iCal program.

Workarounds

All is not lost if your third-party calendar program doesn't export events in the iCal format. Most programs allow you to export calendar events in some format. These files may then be imported into programs that support the iCal format. It can be a pain (depending on which program you're using and which options it gives you for exporting your data), but at least it's possible! Consult your software's documentation for instructions.

Viewing Calendar Entries on Your iPod

Select Extras > Calendars from the main menu. From here you can choose to look at all your calendars or individual calendars. Mac users can also access their to-do lists from this menu. Lastly, you can set the alarm behavior for calendar events: Beep, Silent, or Off.

8:22 PM						
Sun	Mon	Tue	Wed	Thu	Fri	Sat
28	29	30	31	1	2	3
4	5	6	7	8	9	10
11	12	13	14	15	16	17
18	19	20	21	22	23	24
25	26	27	28	29	30	1
2	3	4	5	6	7	8

NOTE: You cannot edit calendar information (or enter new events) on your iPod. Unfortunately, the iPod's calendar feature does not allow for this at this stage in the player's evolution.

19 Notes and Voice Memos

Another of the iPod's exciting PDA features is its ability to store and display notes. With the addition of an aftermarket voice recorder accessory, the full-size iPod can even record voice memos. In Technique 19 we'll introduce the basic note operations of the iPod, then walk you through recording your first voice memo.

Notes

Unfortunately, there is no automatic sync function for transferring notes to your iPod. To use this feature, you'll need to first enable your iPod for disk usage (from the Music tab of the iPod preferences dialog box). Once enabled for disk usage, Mac users will find an icon representing their iPods on their desktops. Windows users will find their iPods listed as removable drives in the My Computer directory.

Notes can be dragged and dropped into the iPod's Notes folder, provided they are saved as plain text files (with a .txt extension). This is a standard text file format, supported by virtually all text-editing programs. Note that there are limits to document length when transferring files; if you have a particularly massive file, you'll need to break it into smaller chunks before you transfer it to your iPod.

▲ The iPod's Notes folder

To view notes on your iPod, navigate to the Extras > Notes directory from the main menu. Highlight the desired file and hit the Select button to view its contents on your screen.

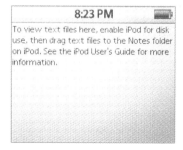

Voice Memos

NOTE: The iPod's voice memo capability is dependent on the use of an aftermarket voice recorder accessory. Unfortunately, at the time of this writing, no such accessory is available for the iPod Nano or iPod Mini. As a result, these iPods are not able to record voice memos.

To enable the iPod's voice memo feature, you will need a compatible voice recorder accessory (see Technique 35 for a suggested product). To record a voice memo, connect your voice recorder accessory to your iPod's Headphones/AV port and select Record from the menu. You can pause recording by pressing the Play/Pause button. Press it again to resume recording. When you're done recording, select Stop, then Save. Your recording will be saved and listed by date and time.

To play a recording back on your iPod, select Extras > Voice Memos. Select the recording you'd like to hear and press Play.

Voice memos are saved in your iPod's Recordings folder in the WAV file format. To transfer voice memos from your iPod to your computer, enable your iPod for disk usage, then drag and drop the files from your iPod's Recordings folder to the desired location of your computer's hard drive. Alternatively, if you have your iPod set to sync automatically, your voice memos will be transferred to your iTunes library the next time you connect your iPod to your computer.

20 Extra Extras—The iPod Nano

The iPod Nano offers a couple of bonus features not found in previous iPod models. If you own a Nano, read on for a brief intro to your iPod's unique extras. iPod and iPod Mini users should check out what they're missing, because they might not be missing these extras for long....

Fingers Crossed!

At the time of this writing, the features described here are only available on the iPod Nano. However, there's always a chance these extras will be added to the iPod and iPod Mini via a software update. Users of these iPods should watch for updates to iPod Updater furiously, just in case Apple decides to share the love. Note that the World Clock feature, described in Technique 16, is also exclusive to the Nano at this time.

Stopwatch

With its absurdly small size and undetectable weight, the iPod Nano is the perfect music player for working out—so it's only natural that Apple gave it a stopwatch feature. To access the Nano's stopwatch, navigate to Extras > Stopwatch from the main menu.

Select Timer from the Stopwatch menu to bring up the stopwatch itself. Highlight and select Start to start the clock.

Press the Lap button to record your lap times. Your total time is displayed above the time for your current lap.

Click Pause to stop the clock, then click Resume or Done to either continue your workout or call it a day.

Note that your stopwatch will continue to run if you back out of its menu and do other things with your iPod. Simply return to the stopwatch when you're ready to view your results or issue a new command.

Once you finish a stopwatch session, your result are saved automatically in the Extras > Stopwatch menu. Entries are listed by date and time. Select a stopwatch session to view data relevant to that session. Your total time; shortest, longest, and average lap times; as well as the individual times for each of your laps are stored for your review.

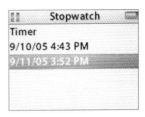

Screen Lock

For the benefit of iPod Nano users who demand a little security for their players, Apple has added a screen lock feature to the Extras menu. By selecting a four-digit security code for your iPod, you can keep others from listening to your music or viewing your personal data without your permission.

To select your code, start at the main menu and select Extras > Screen Lock > Set Combination. Use the Click Wheel to dial in the first digit, then hit the Select button or the Next/Fast-forward button to proceed to the next. Hit the Previous/Rewind button to back up to a previous digit. With your code entered, hit the Select button while the fourth digit is highlighted to save your code and return to the Screen Lock menu.

To lock your screen, select Turn Screen Lock On from the Screen Lock menu, read the helpful warning, and select Lock from the menu. Your iPod will now display its combination lock until you enter the correct unlock code.

Unlock your screen by entering the correct code (using the same procedure given previously). If this fails, or if you forget your code, simply connect your Nano to your primary computer; it will unlock as soon as it mounts to your system. If this doesn't work (for some reason), see Technique 38 for instructions for restoring your Nano's software to its factory state. It's a dramatic step, and it will delete all your data, but it's your fault for forgetting that stupid code!

Chapter 3

21

Third-Party Software

The iPod's suite of extra features has created a market for third-party software dedicated to improving these functions. In addition to offering alternatives to Apple's software, these programs often bring entirely new (and unique) functionality to the iPod party. In this section, we'll introduce a few of the better programs available on the Mac and Windows platforms.

Recommended Mac Software

Senuti: Apple, no doubt in the interest of making suppliers of music to the iTMS happy, developed iTunes so that you cannot copy tracks from your iPod into your iTunes library. Though this might frustrate would-be music pirates, it also bums out those of us who lose our iTunes libraries to dead hard drives, only to find there is no way to recover these files from our iPods. Needless to say, third-party developers have stepped in to fill the void. Senuti is one of the better programs offering this functionality.

http://wbyoung.ambitiouslemon.com/senuti/

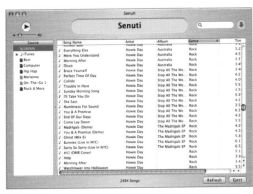

▲ Senuti

Pod2Go: Pod2Go is a great program for stuffing your iPod with information. Use it to find and transfer news, weather info, movie times, and even driving directions to your iPod (using the built-in notes feature).

http://www.kainjow.com/pod2go/

▲ Pod2Go

Book2Pod: The iPod's note feature is great, but it's restricted by a size limit imposed on note files. Book2Pod cleverly formats larger text documents so they will work with your iPod, bypassing this limitation.

http://www.tomsci.com/book2pod/

iSpeak It: A number of programs download news feeds directly to your iPod. The interesting thing about iSpeak is that it filters text documents through your Mac's text-to-speech software to create spoken-word audio tracks. In other words, you can listen to printed news on your iPod rather than read it!

http://www.zapptek.com/ispeak-it/

▲ iSpeak It

iPod It: In addition to retrieving news and weather info for your iPod, iPod It expands your iPod's PDA-like sync capabilities. For this author, the must-have feature here is support for Microsoft Entourage contacts and calendar events.

http://www.zapptek.com/ipod-it/

▲ iPod It

Recommended Windows Software

PodPlus: PodPlus offers a staggering number of features in one package. Like Senuti for the Mac, it lets you transfer songs from your iPod back into iTunes (in case your computer's hard drive dies). It also syncs Microsoft Outlook information and loads your iPod with a wild assortment of Web-based info (news feeds, weather info, movie show times, etc.).

http://www.ipodsoft.com/index.php?/software/podplus

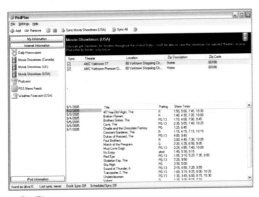

▲ PodPlus

iPodSync: Windows user lack something Mac users have in Apple's iSync program: an all-in-one solution for syncing data between their computers and iPods. iPodSync fills this gap nicely for PC users.

http://www.ipod-sync.com/

XPlay: Xplay offers a suite of exciting features, including the ability to transfer songs from your iPod to your computer. But its most impressive feature is that it allows Mac-formatted iPods to operate seamlessly with Windows PCs—without the need for reformatting!

http://www.mediafour.com/products/xplay/

▲ XPlay

Anapod Explorer: No list of Windows iPod software would be complete without Anapod Explorer. This feature-laden program offers an alternate to the iTunes experience. For those iPod users who just can't get into iTunes, Anapod Explorer offers a way to access all of your iPod's features without using Apple's software. Best of all, Anapod Explorer allows you to transcode audio on the fly during song transfers. Sadly, you can't say that about iTunes!

http://www.redchairsoftware.com/anapod/

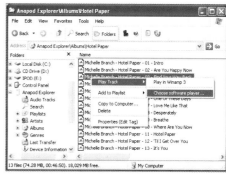

▲ Anapod Explorer

40 iPod Techniques

One Hard Drive, to Go

One of the great benefits to owning an iPod is that, in addition to being an incredible MP3 player, it doubles as a portable hard drive. With capacities sufficient to transfer substantial file loads, iPods can work just as much as they play.

In Chapter 4 we'll illustrate your iPod's hard-drive talents, then cover some of the nifty things you can do to exploit this functionality.

22

Using the iPod as a Portable Hard Drive

To get things rolling, we'll cover setting up and using your iPod as a drive. We'll also discuss the limitations that affect your iPod's use as an external hard drive.

Basic Disk Operations

1. Open iTunes and select your iPod in the Source list. Click the "Display iPod options" button at the lower right of the iTunes window to bring up the iPod preferences dialog box. (Alternatively, right-click or Ctrl-click the iPod icon in the Source list and select iPod Options from the pop-up menu.)

2. Select the Music tab, then check the "Enable disk use" check box. Click OK. Note that if you are manually managing your music, the disk usage option will be enabled by default.

3. Close or hide iTunes. Mac users will see the iPod as an icon on the desktop. Windows users can access the iPod in the My Computer folder (accessible from the Start menu). Double-click the iPod icon to open a window showing your iPod's contents. Notice that your music files are not accessible here; this is an anti-piracy measure adopted by Apple in the interest of playing nice with the recording industry. As we covered in the previous chapter, you can access your Calendars, Contacts, and Notes folders from your iPod's root directory. Users of the iPod and iPod Nano will also have a Photos folder (provided there are photos currently on your iPod).

4. To use your iPod as a hard drive, simply drag and drop files to and from the iPod's folder or icon. To delete files from your iPod, drag them to the Trash or Recycle Bin as you would any other computer file.

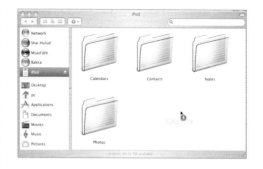

As with using your iPod in iTunes, it's important to eject your iPod from your computer prior to disconnecting it physically. To do this, right-click (or Ctrl-click) the iPod icon and select Eject from the pop-up menu. Mac users also have the option of dragging the iPod icon to the Trash. Windows users have the option of clicking the Safely Remove Hardware icon in the system tray at the bottom of their screens.

Mac users can check the iPod's free drive space by double-clicking the iPod icon to open its contents window. The available drive space is shown at the bottom of the file window. Windows users can right-click the iPod icon and select Properties from the pop-up menu.

Cross-Platform Disk Usage

iPods formatted for use on PCs and Macs use different hard-drive formatting standards. Fortunately for Mac users, Mac OS X is capable of recognizing the Windows drive format, so Windows-formatted iPods will mount to the Mac desktop. From there, for the most part, you can use your iPod just as you would a Mac-formatted iPod. The main limitation you must be aware of is that the Windows drive format does not allow certain special characters to be used in file names. Files using these characters will not transfer to a Windows-formatted iPod connected to a Mac. The characters in question follow:

\ / : * ? " < > |

Windows users are not so lucky. A Mac-formatted iPod will not mount to a Windows PC. If you attempt this, your PC will ask your permission to reformat your iPod. Fortunately, there are third-party utilities available that allow PCs to mount Mac-formatted iPods. See the listing for Xplay in Technique 21 for details.

Power User's Tip

If you plan to use your iPod as a portable drive extensively, you may want to deselect the "Open iTunes when this iPod is attached" option from the iPod preferences dialog box. Otherwise, it might become annoying to have iTunes jump up every time you're trying to do a simple file transfer.

23

Transferring Your iTunes Library to Another Computer

One of the best ways to use your iPod as a hard drive is to transfer your music to a new computer. Though you can't do this through iTunes (without the aid of third-party software), it is possible! In this section we'll walk you through the process.

Transferring Audio

1. A good place to start is with consolidating your library in iTunes (if it isn't already). You may have audio files listed in iTunes that are scattered randomly throughout your computer's hard-drive directory. Consolidating your library will copy all of the music files listed in iTunes into the iTunes library folder on your computer. To consolidate your library, select Consolidate Library from the Advanced menu in the iTunes menu bar.

Consolidating your library will copy all of your music into the iTunes Music folder.

This cannot be undone.

Cancel   Consolidate

2. With your iPod enabled for disk usage (see Technique 22), locate your iTunes library folder on your computer and drag it onto your iPod. By default, Mac users will find their library folder at [Startup drive] > Users > [User name] > Music > iTunes > iTunes Music. PC users can find theirs at C:\Documents and Settings\[User name]\My Documents\My Music\iTunes\iTunes Music. Note that you'll need enough free space on your iPod to store these files. If you lack sufficient space, you might consider deleting files from your iPod temporarily to facilitate the move. Alternatively, you can transfer audio files to your new computer in several batches.

3. Eject your iPod, disconnect if from your computer, and attach it to the destination computer. If you're moving your tunes from a Mac to a PC (or vice versa), see our note about cross-platform disk usage in Technique 22.

4. Open iTunes and select Preferences from the iTunes (Mac) or Edit (PC) menu. Select the Advanced tab and check the "Copy files to iTunes Music folder when adding to library" option.

5. Double-click your iPod to open its contents window. Size and arrange both this window and your iTunes window so that you can access both at once. Now drag and drop your library folder from your iPod into the iTunes Track frame. Your tracks will be added to the iTunes library, and their associated files will be copied to your new computer's designated library folder. This may take a while, depending on the size of your library, so be patient!

Transferring Playlists

You may have noticed that the technique given above doesn't mention your playlists! To transfer these to your new library, perform the following steps:

1. Start by exporting your playlists from your old version of iTunes. To do this, highlight the desired playlist in the Source list and select Export Song List from the File menu. Save the playlist directly to your iPod (you'll need to have it connected to your computer, of course). Repeat this step for each of your playlists.

2. Eject and disconnect your iPod, then connect it to your new computer.

3. After you've imported your audio into iTunes using the steps given previously, select Import from the File menu. From the Import dialog box, select a playlist file on your iPod. Click Choose, and your old playlist will be added to your new iTunes library. Repeat this step for each of the playlists stored on your iPod.

40 iPod Techniques

Photos on the Run

Apple no longer sells iPods that lack photo functionality. (Well, there's the Shuffle, but that doesn't count!) Even iPod Nano users (as tiny as the Nano is) can enjoy an assortment of full-color photo features.

In Chapter 5 we'll walk you through your iPod's photo features, then wrap up by demonstrating how you can use your iPod as a portable hard drive for your digital camera.

24

Chapter 5

Transferring Photos to and from Your iPod

First things first: we've got to get your photos onto your iPod. In Technique 24, we'll illustrate the steps for both Mac and Windows users.

Supported Image Formats

Before you explore your iPod's photo features, it's important to note the image file formats it supports: BMP, GIF, JPEG, PNG, PSD (Mac-formatted iPods only), and TIFF.

Syncing to a Photo Application—Mac Users

Mac users who manage their digital photos with Apple's iPhoto program (version 4.0.3 or later) benefit from some of the same automated sync features that control their iCal and Address Book information.

1. With your iPod connected to your computer, right-click (or Ctrl-click) its icon in the iTunes Source list and select iPod Options from the pop-up menu.

2. Select the Photo tab and check the "Synchronize photos from" box. Select iPhoto from the pull-down menu. You may then choose whether to mirror your entire iPhoto library or only specific albums.

3. Click OK, and your iPod will begin transferring photos. Note that this may take some time if you have a lot of photos. On subsequent syncs, changes made to your iPhoto library will be reflected on your iPod automatically.

Syncing to a Photo Application—Windows Users

Windows users, though they lack Apple's iPhoto application, can still experience its benefits—provided they have Adobe Photoshop Album (version 1.0 or later) or Adobe Photoshop Elements (version 3.0 or later) installed.

1. With your iPod connected to your computer, right-click its icon in the iTunes Source list and select iPod Options from the pop-up menu.

2. Select the Photo tab and check the "Synchronize photos from" box. Select Photoshop Album or Photoshop Elements from the pull-down menu. You may then choose whether to mirror all the photos associated with these programs or only certain collections. (If your version doesn't support collections, you can still choose to import everything.)

3. Click OK, and your iPod will begin transferring photos. Note that this may take some time if you have a lot of photos. On subsequent syncs, changes made to your collections will be reflected on your iPod automatically.

Syncing to a Folder

Mac and Windows users also have the option of syncing the iPod to a folder containing photos on their computers' hard drive.

1. Bring up your iPod's preferences in iTunes and check the "Synchronize photos from" option. This time, select the Choose Folder option from the pull-down menu. Select a folder from the dialog box and click Choose. Again, you can choose to sync to the entire contents of your photo folder or to specific subfolders contained within it.

2. Click OK, and your iPod will begin transferring photos. On subsequent syncs, changes made to your selected folder(s) will be reflected on your iPod automatically.

ncluding Full-Resolution Photos

By default, photos transferred to your iPod are optimized (i.e., compressed) so that they consume a minimal amount of space on your iPod. These images look great on your iPod's relatively small screen, but if you have other purposes in mind—such as transferring photos to another computer—you'll want to transfer full-resolution images to your iPod. To do this, check the "Include full-resolution photos" box on the Photos tab of the iPod preferences dialog box.

Transferring Photos from Your iPod to Your Computer

If you enable the full-resolution photos option for your iPod, images transferred to your iPod will appear in your iPod's Photos > Full Resolution folder. To transfer these files to another computer, follow these steps:

1. With your iPod loaded with full-resolution photos, connect it to the destination computer.

2. If your iPod isn't already enabled for disk usage, open iTunes and check the "Enable disk use" box on the Music tab of your iPod preferences.

3. Open your iPod's contents window from the desktop (Mac) or My Computer directory (PC) and navigate to the Photos > Full Resolution folder.

4. Drag and drop your Full Resolution folder to the desired location on the destination computer. (See Technique 22 for additional details related to using your iPod as a portable hard drive.)

25 Viewing Photos on Your iPod

Once you've got photos on your iPod, there are a number of ways you can enjoy them there. In this section, we'll illustrate what your iPod can do once it's loaded with your favorite images.

Viewing Photos Manually

1. To view images on your iPod, choose Photos > Photo Library from your iPod's main menu. Alternatively, choose a specific album from the Photos menu to view images from that photo album.

2. Once you've chosen your photo library or album, you'll see thumbnails for the images contained within. Use the Click Wheel to choose the image you want to display, then press the Select button to view it on-screen.

3. Use the Next/Fast-forward and Previous/Rewind buttons to maneuver through your photos. Alternatively, use the Click Wheel to cycle through your images.

4. When you're done viewing photos, click the Menu button to return to the iPod's menu interface. Click it several times to return to the main menu.

Viewing Slideshows on Your iPod

You can also view slideshows of the images on your iPod and even set these to music. Follow the steps below to set this feature up:

1. To get started, select Slideshow Settings from your iPod's Photos menu.

2. From here, set the parameters that control your iPod slideshow, including the time each slide is shown and the music you'd like to play during the show. One particularly cool feature is the Transitions menu, which allows you to specify a visual effect for the transitions between slides.

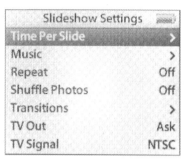

3. With your parameters selected, return to the Photos menu and highlight your photo library (or album of choice). There are several ways to initiate a slideshow. First, you can highlight your library or an individual album and press the Play button. Alternatively, navigate to the thumbnail screen for your library (or album of choice) and press the Play button on the photo you'd like to start the slideshow with. Finally, you can select an individual image from the thumbnail screen and then hit the Select button when the image is shown full-screen on your iPod.

4. By default, your iPod is set to ask whether you're outputting your slideshow to a TV for viewing. To view the slideshow on your iPod, select the TV Off option. Additional info on the iPod's TV-out capabilities can be found in Technique 26.

5. Press the Play button to pause during a slideshow, and press it again to resume. Use the Next/Fast-forward and Previous/Rewind buttons to skip through your photos manually. Press the Menu button to exit the slideshow screen and return to your iPod's menu.

26

Connecting Your iPod to Your TV

Though the procedure requires some extra hardware and a compatible television, viewing iPod slideshows on you TV. is one of the cooler things your iPod can do. In Technique 26, we'll show you the ropes.

Note that, although it supports photo features, the iPod Nano does not support TV-out functionality at the time of this writing.

There are a few basic things you'll need to view iPod photos on your TV. These accessories are all available through Apple-licensed retailers.

Option 1 requirements: Apple's iPod AV Cable. A television with RCA audio inputs is required for sound.

Option 2 requirements: Apple's iPod AV Cable and Apple's iPod Dock. A television with RCA audio inputs is required for sound.

Option 3 requirements: Apple's iPod Dock, an S-Video cable, and a splitter cable with a 3.5 mm stereo mini-plug at one end and dual RCA outputs at the other. A television with RCA audio inputs is required for sound.

To set up option 1, plug the iPod AV Cable's mini-plug into your iPod's Headphones/AV port, then plug the audio/video cables into your TV set (yellow = video, red = right stereo channel, and white = left stereo channel).

For option 2, dock your iPod, plug the iPod AV Cable's mini-plug into the Line Out port of your dock, and plug the audio/video cables into your TV as described previously.

▲ An iPod with the iPod AV Cable

For option 3, dock your iPod, plug the mini-plug end of your audio cable into the dock's Line Out port, and plug the red and white RCA cables into the right and left audio inputs of your TV, respectively. Finally, plug the S-Video cable into your dock on one end and your TV's S-Video input on the other.

With your iPod connected to your TV, simply view a slideshow from your iPod using the method described in Technique 25. Everything will be piped into your TV. (Note that when you view a slideshow on a television set, your iPod will not mirror exactly what's showing on the big screen.)

There are a couple of slideshow settings that apply specifically to viewing photos on your television. First, make sure your iPod's TV Out feature is set to On. (By default, you'll be asked whether and you're outputting to a TV each time you play a slideshow.) You can also toggle the TV Signal option between NTSC or PAL.

NTSC and PAL are different signal technologies that are used for televisions in different regions of the world. Generally speaking, North America, Central America, and northern/western South America, as well as Japan and South Korea, use the NTSC standard. Southern/eastern South America, much of Africa, Australia, and most European nations use the PAL standard. By default your iPod is set to the signal standard used by the country in which you purchased your iPod, so it's unlikely you'll have to worry about this. However, if you travel internationally, this option may come in quite handy!

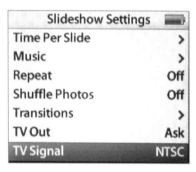

When your slideshow ends, the last image will remain on-screen and the music will continue to play. Press the Menu button on your iPod and select your next slideshow!

27

Using the iPod with a Digital Camera

While it does not come with iPods, Apple's iPod Camera Connector is a worthy add-on. The Camera Connector lets you import photos from a digital camera directly to your iPod. For Technique 27, we'll show you the ropes of your iPod's digital-camera features. Note that, although it supports photo features, the iPod Nano does not support importing images from digital cameras at the time of this writing.

Your camera and your iPod are going to be best friends. With its photos tucked safely into your iPod, your camera's memory card can be erased and filled anew. By offering this feature, your iPod pulls double duty, acting not only as a brilliant MP3 player but also as an in-the-field storage device for your digital camera. You can even view imported photos on your iPod then transfer them directly to your computer for storage or processing. Have a 60 GB iPod? You won't need another flash card for your camera...ever.

Transferring Photos from a Camera to Your iPod

1. Check that both your digital camera and your iPod are charged. Turn on your camera and set it to its display/export mode. (See your camera's documentation for instructions.)

2. Connect the camera to the iPod Camera Connector via USB cable. If your camera did not come with one, you will need to purchase a USB cable for this operation.

3. Plug in the iPod Camera Connector to your iPod and select Import when prompted. When the import process is complete, your photos will be listed on your iPod by roll number.

If your camera has the ability to record videos, your iPod can import these through the iPod Camera Connector. However, you will not be able to view videos on your iPod. (It's widely speculated that video is coming to the iPod soon, so maybe this will be an option in the near future.)

iewing Imported Photos on Your Pod

To view imported photos, scroll to Photos > Photo Import and select which roll or rolls you wish to view, then choose Browse to display the corresponding photos. You can also delete photo rolls from your iPod if you decide they aren't worth keeping.

Note that you will not be able to view imported photos in a slideshow on your iPod. To view imported photos in a slideshow, you must first transfer them to your computer and then reimport them to your iPod as "regular" iPod images.

Transferring Imported Photos from Your iPod to Your Computer

When you import photos directly to your iPod, a DCIM folder is created in your iPod's hard-drive directory. If your iPod is enabled for disk use, you can simply plug it into your computer and drag and drop these files to your desktop (or any other destination on your computer).

Alternatively, you can import the contents of the DCIM folder into your photo-editing application of choice. Most applications treat the iPod as if it were a digital camera.

40 iPod Techniques

Do the Shuffle

The iPod Shuffle provides iPod devotees with a less expensive, more durable, ultraportable iPod option. Though it lacks an LCD screen and many of the other iPods' extra features, the Shuffle's ease of use and unique on-the-go functionality make it a great option if one of the larger iPods are simply too expensive or too big to capture your interest. The Shuffle also makes a great second MP3 player—a perfect "low-key" companion for your bulky (by comparison) 60 GB player.

In this chapter we'll introduce the iPod Shuffle hardware and walk you through the ins and outs of running the device. We'll wrap up by providing instructions for using your Shuffle as a portable storage device.

28 Welcome to the Shuffle

Though there are two versions of the iPod Shuffle (512 MB and 1 GB), their designs and operations are identical. To get things started, we'll illustrate the controls and basic functions of your new Shuffle.

iPod Shuffle Hardware

Unlike the iPod and iPod Mini, which use hard drives similar to your computer's (only smaller), the Nano and Shuffle use flash memory to store your music. The benefit of flash-based devices is that they have no moving parts. As a result, they are less susceptible to shock-related damage and they never skip during music playback.

The biggest thing you'll notice about the Shuffle is its lack of an LCD screen. In spite of this (or maybe because of it), the controls on the front of the Shuffle are intuitive and easy to use. Play, pause, skip, repeat, shuffle, and hold functions can be selected with a touch of your thumb. See the following list for a complete overview of the Shuffle's controls.

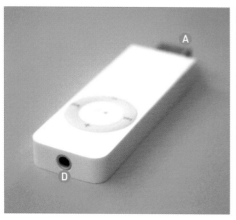

A. **USB connector**: The USB connector is the Shuffle's equivalent of the Dock Connector port found on other iPods. Plug the USB connector into your computer's USB port to charge the Shuffle's battery and transfer music and files. The Shuffle can connect to a Mac or PC through a high-power USB or USB 2.0 port, and—unlike other iPod models—it can move between Macs and PCs freely.

B. **Transport and volume controls**: The Shuffle's panel of buttons, though it lacks the "neat-o" factor of the Click Wheel, provides a convenient assortment of playback controls.

C. **Status light**: The status light glows green for a few seconds when you turn your Shuffle on. It also flashes green whenever you issue a button command. If you pause during music playback, the light will flash green for one minute. The light glows amber while your Shuffle is charging and switches to green when the battery is fully charged. If your Shuffle is being used as a disk, the amber light blinks on and off. If you press and hold the Play button for about three seconds, the status light flashes amber three times to indicate that you're in Hold mode. In this state your iPod's controls are frozen to protect against unintentional button presses. Press and hold Play again to release Hold mode.

D. **Headphone port**: As you might expect, plug your headphones in here!

E. **Battery status button/light**: This light glows amber while your iPod is charging, and green when the battery is fully charged. The battery status light blinks amber when your Shuffle is being used as a disk. Press the button to receive feedback regarding your battery level: red indicates a low charge, amber indicates a moderate charge, and green indicates a high charge level. If no light appears, the battery is completely drained.

F. **Power switch**: The power switch has three positions. The topmost position is off. The middle position turns your Shuffle on and instructs it to play tracks in sequential order. The final position powers up your Shuffle and initiates random play.

Basic Shuffle Operations

- To start playing a track, press the Play/Pause button once.

- To pause, press the Play/Pause button once. To resume play, press it again.

- To go to the beginning of the playlist, quickly press the Play/Pause button three times.

- To skip to the next track, press the Next/Fast-forward button once. To return to the beginning of the current track, press the Previous/Rewind button once. To go back to the previous track, press the Previous/Rewind button twice quickly.

- To adjust the volume, press the Volume Up (+) button and the Volume Down (-) button.

- To enter Hold mode, press and hold the Play/Pause button for about three seconds. To exit Hold mode, press and hold the Play/Pause button for another three seconds.

Troubleshooting the Shuffle

If the status light flashes green and amber, it means there is a problem—music won't play on your Shuffle. Try turning the Shuffle off and on again. If the light persists, connect it to iTunes and reload your music.

If the problem continues, visit http://www.apple.com and make sure you have the latest iPod software. You may have to reformat your Shuffle to update its firmware. See Technique 38 for instructions.

If the problem persists, there's little else to do other than contact Apple's customer service and review the details of your warranty.

29 Advanced Shuffle Operations

The procedure for syncing the iPod Shuffle with iTunes is different than it is with the other iPods. In this section, we'll walk you through the process for maintaining a healthy rotation of tracks on your Shuffle.

Plug It In

Due to the limited feature set and playback operations of the Shuffle, it's assumed that it will be used for quick, on-the-go playback of random tracks. To make song selection and syncing as efficient as possible, iTunes provides a streamlined interface for loading the Shuffle with tunes.

The first time you connect the Shuffle to a free USB port on your computer, iTunes launches automatically and the iPod Setup Assistant pops up. You'll be asked at this point whether you want iTunes to automatically fill the Shuffle with a random assortment of songs. If you leave this option selected, your Shuffle will begin filling up on tracks as soon as you exit the setup assistant.

An icon representing your Shuffle will appear in the Source list as soon as iTunes finishes mounting the device. Whenever tracks are being copied to your Shuffle, its icon will flash red.

▲ The iPod Setup Assistant dialog box

Using the Autofill Feature

When your iPod is selected in the Source list, the Autofill frame will appear at the bottom of the Track frame. The Autofill feature fills your iPod with tracks based on a few criteria. You can specify where tracks are drawn from (between your entire library, playlist folders, or individual playlists) and choose from a few basic guidelines that determine how tracks are selected. You can also specify whether you want all the tracks on your Shuffle to be replaced each time you give the Autofill command.

▲ Specifying a playlist from the autofill pull down menu

Manual Transfers

As with the other iPods, you also have the option of operating your Shuffle manually. There's no need to use the iPod preferences dialog box to set the Shuffle to manual, however, as it operates manually by default. Simply drag and drop songs, playlists, or playlist folders to the Shuffle icon in the Source list to add them to the Shuffle.

▲ The "not enough free space" warning dialog box

If you select more songs than you have room for on your Shuffle, iTunes will alert you to this and fill the Shuffle with as many of your selected tracks as it can. To delete tracks from the Shuffle, highlight the desired track(s), right-click (or Ctrl-click), and select Clear from the pop-up menu.

Shuffle Preferences

Right-click (or Ctrl-click) the Shuffle icon in the Source list and select iPod preferences from the pop-up menu to access your Shuffle's preference settings. Most of these options are quite straightforward (the Shuffle is not a complicated device), but two warrant further discussion.

▲ The Shuffle's unique preferences dialog box

If you select the "Keep this iPod in the source list" option, your Shuffle will remain selectable in the Source list even if you eject it from iTunes. The listing basically acts as a playlist, mirroring your Shuffle's contents. You can even play tracks from here (again, even if your Shuffle is disconnected). What's really cool about it, though, is that any changes you make to this "playlist" will be made to your Shuffle the next time you connect it. In other words, you can plan your Shuffle's next fill-up without connecting it to your computer.

If you select the "Convert higher bit rate songs to 128 kbps AAC for this iPod" option, iTunes will do exactly that when you autofill your Shuffle. And don't worry—your original library tracks will not be harmed in the process. If you've read Technique 11, which discusses the process of transcoding audio files, you know the hoops users of the iPod, iPod Nano, and iPod Mini must jump through to manually convert tracks to reduce their file sizes. Let's cross our fingers and hope that Apple provides this functionality for other iPod models in the future!

30

Using the Shuffle as a Flash Drive

You might have noticed the recent craze created by tiny USB "thumb" drives. Capable of surprisingly large storage capacities, these miniscule, lightweight devices allow for significant file exchanges in a featherweight package. Not to be outdone, Apple has included this functionality in the iPod Shuffle. In Technique 30 we'll show you how to use your Shuffle as a portable storage device.

Enabling Disk Usage

As with the iPod, iPod Nano, and iPod Mini, the Shuffle can be used as a portable storage device. Without any wires to worry about, or any compatibility issues when moving between Macs and PCs, the Shuffle is a great way to store and transfer relatively small batches of files.

By default, the Shuffle's disk usage option is disabled; it'll only play music out of the box. To enable its use as a portable drive, plug it into a free USB port and open iTunes. Bring up the iPod preferences dialog box and select the "Enable disk use" option. Use the slider to determine how much of the Shuffle's storage capacity will be reserved for disk usage—weigh songs on the left against data capacity on the right.

▲ Enabling the Shuffle for disk use

Note that if you already have songs on your Shuffle and you select a disk capacity that is larger than your available space, iTunes will automatically delete songs to free up the appropriate amount of space (assuming you give it the OK to do so).

▲ The "make room for data" warning dialog box

If you plan to use the Shuffle as a portable drive extensively, you may want to deselect the "Open iTunes when this iPod is attached" option from the iPod preferences dialog box. Otherwise, it might become annoying having iTunes jump up every time you're trying to do a simple file transfer.

Once your Shuffle is enabled for disk usage, it appears on your computer as any other portable storage device would.

Transferring Files

Mac users will see their Shuffle on their desktop. Windows users will find it in their My Computer directory. Double-click your Shuffle's icon to open a folder showing its contents. Drag and drop items to and from the folder to add or remove them from the Shuffle. Right-click (or Ctrl-click) and select Eject from the pop-up menu to safely remove the Shuffle from your system. Once ejected, you can pull the Shuffle from its USB slot.

▲ Transferring files to the Shuffle

To transfer files to another computer, simply plug it in as you normally would. If there is an iTunes library on the new computer, you will be given a prompt asking if you'd like to link the Shuffle to that library (rather than its currently linked library). Click No to keep the alternate version of iTunes from interfering with the contents of your Shuffle.

▲ The "change the link" dialog box

40 iPod Techniques

Accessories Make the iPod

The great success of the iPod has, not surprisingly, created a huge market for accessories and add-ons. From the more mundane (cases and audio hookups) to the more inspired (microphones and car stereo adapters), there are countless accessories that allow you to customize and upgrade your iPod.

In Chapter 7 we'll discuss some of the things to look for while shopping for iPod accessories. We'll also show you what your iPod can do with the aid of aftermarket add-ons.

Note that, as the iPod Nano is brand new, there are very few accessories available for it at the time of this writing. However, many of the principles discussed in this chapters will be valuable to Nano owners. Also, many of the accessories listed are not dependent on the use of a specific iPod model, so Nano users can adopt these "legacy" products for use with their players.

31   A Case for Cases

A case is a case. Though this is true to some extent, you wouldn't know it by the insane number of options on the market. To get things rolling, we'll discuss some of the things you should look for in an iPod case, then provide a list of recommended products.

Use your iPod for about 20 seconds and you'll notice what so many of us have: these things love to pick up scratches. Though the Shuffle is somewhat immune due to the plastic used for its housing, the iPod, iPod Nano, and iPod Mini are all prime candidates for a truckload of scratches.

There's also the matter of shock damage. Hard-drive-based models (iPod and Mini) are more vulnerable than flash-based models (Nano and Shuffle), but no matter what iPod you own, it's a bad idea to smack it around.

In short, it's smart to get a case for your iPod. Here's are some things to watch out for when making your selection:

Cooling issues: Your iPod's case is designed to dissipate heat that can result from its operations or from charging its battery. Strapping a tight case around your iPod can interfere with its cooling capabilities. Since heat is one of your iPod's battery's worst enemies, this isn't good! Fortunately, some cases are designed so that heat can still dissipate from your iPod effectively. Other cases simply aren't designed to fully encase your iPod, and these too are usually a safe bet. Note that, regardless of what case you buy, Apple recommends removing it prior to charging your iPod just to play it safe.

Screen protection: Many cases fail to offer protection for your iPod's screen. This is ironic, since the face of your iPod's screen is both the most vulnerable location on your iPod and—if damaged—has the greatest potential to ruin your iPod. It's not a lot of fun to look at photos on your iPod if your screen is dull and loaded with scratches! We recommend that you look for cases that offer screen protection of some kind, preferably in the form of a hard plastic, transparent cover that sits over your iPod's screen.

Materials: Though iPod cases come in a variety of materials (from leather to hard plastic), this author has a clear preference: rubber. Rubber cases often come in sharp, "high-tech" colors, they feel great to the touch, and they offer rudimentary shock absorption should you drop your iPod from a reasonably low height. Granted, they also have a reputation for picking up lint and hair like double-sided tape, but it's a small price to pay for peace of mind.

Dock interference: There is one huge drawback to most iPod cases: they obstruct the top and bottom of your iPod. At the bottom of your iPod, the Dock Connector port allows you to connect your iPod to your computer or an iPod docking apparatus (these include not only computer docks but also stereos that feature iPod mounts). Most cases allow you to plug a FireWire or USB cable into the Dock Connector port, but—by enclosing the bottom of your iPod— they preclude the use of any kind of dock. Maddeningly, you must undress your iPod prior to docking it. Though no case maker is foolish enough to obstruct the Headphone/AV port of your iPod, many accessories are designed to fit snugly on the top of your iPod. By enclosing the top of your iPod, your case impedes the use of such accessories. Again, you'll have to remove your case prior to using these add-ons.

Recommended Cases

NOTE: Prices are current list prices at the time of this writing.

All iPod Models: iPod Socks, Apple, $29

Cute and cuddly, these socks protect the iPod from basic mishaps while keeping an air of whimsy. These are perfect for students, but professionals may want to steer clear.

http://www.apple.com

iPod Nano: iPod Nano Tubes, Apple, $29

The iPod Nano is still brand new at the time of this writing, but Apple was kind enough to release this case simultaneously with the Nano. Made of filth-resistant silicone, it even offers protection for your Nano's Click Wheel.

http://www.apple.com

iPod Mini: SV iMini, H20 Audio, $150

The manufacturer (H20 Audio) claims this case will protect your iPod Mini under water at depths up to 10 feet. It's up to you whether you need tunes while you're swimming in a reef. This is perfect for mermaids, lifeguards, and wealthy beach bums.

http://www.h2oaudio.com/index.php

iPod and iPod Mini: Sleevz for iPod, Radtech, $20.95 (iPod), 18.95 (iPod Mini)

Made of Optex fiber, this snug cocoon keeps your iPod free of scratches. You can control your iPod through the material, so even your Click Wheel gets to hide beneath this skin. (It won't exactly protect iPod from a fall, however.) This is perfect for those who baby their iPods.

http://www.radtech.us/

iPod, iPod Mini, iPod Shuffle, iPod Nano: iPod skins (various models), iSkin, prices vary

Tough, resilient, and offered in several cool designs, iSkin cases will protect your iPod from a tumble here and there while keeping the scratches at bay. These are perfect for those who need a little extra protection.

http://www.iskin.com/

iPod, iPod Mini, iPod Shuffle, iPod Nano: Leather cases (various models), Vaja, prices vary

Vaja makes several very stylish, very robust cases for each of the iPod models. Though the sticker price (upwards of $75) may put you off, these are definitely some slick cases.

http://www.vajacases.com/home_en.html

32   Headphones

If you're using the iPod for what it's designed to do (take your music on the road), you're getting a lot of use out of your headphones. In this section, we'll mention a few things to watch for when you're shopping for headphones, then recommend some products.

Most people agree that the headphones packaged with iPods are weak. Apple clearly considers the iPod to be the star of the show, and the disrespect they show their stock headphones is evident. The last thing you want to do is spend a chunk of money (as much as $399!) on a fancy new iPod and then languish under the yoke of tinny, uncomfortable ear buds.

The importance of aftermarket headphones has increased recently due to iPod-related crime waves. Basically, thieves know that Apple's ear buds are usually connected to very high-resale-value iPods. As a result, they've developed a taste for snatching iPods based on this identification.

To get you on the right path to a decent set of phones, consider the following:

Comfort: Comfort is an issue that a lot of people ignore when shopping for headphones, and they often live to regret their carelessness. It's likely that your headphones are going to be on your head for pretty good stretches of time, and no matter how good they sound, they're going to be awful if they make you want to claw your ears off. Of course, comfort is a very personal sense, so we can't offer a specific recommendation here. Just know that there are quite a few basic form factors on the market—over-the-head, behind-the-neck, enclosed, open-air, ear bud, around-the-ear, etc.—and it's a good idea to pay close attention to the way a set of headphones is going to sit on your head. If it looks uncomfortable, it probably is.

Frequency range: Generally, it's accepted that the human ear can process sound in the 20 to 20,000 Hz range. Headphones (and speakers, for that matter) are always rated according to their possible frequency range. Look for headphones that cover the 20 to 20,000Hz range to ensure transparent sound reproduction with maximum clarity. The low end of that range (20 Hz) represents bass frequencies, so for those of you who prefer a full but unmuddied bass sound, make sure your headphones have the bottom end covered.

Cord and jack: There are several technologies that can be employed to ensure the best connection between your iPod and your ears. Cords and audio plugs are often marketed to trumpet the quality of their components and designs. After all, an audio signal is only as good as the path it travels along. Look for marketing that boasts about the quality of these components—oxygen-free copper, shielding, gold plating, etc.

Tangle-free cords: Anyone with a short history using consumer electronics knows what a pain it is to untangle knotted cords. Some headphone manufacturers are including "tangle-free" cords with their products. This is something to look for if you're prone to creating snake pits.

Portability: It's a basic thing, but it's still important: look for headphones that fold up and/or include a carrying case if you plan to get a lot of road use out of them.

Recommended Headphones

NOTE: Prices are current list prices at the time of this writing.

Earbuds: In-Ear Headphones, Apple, $39

Offering a better fit and sound quality than the in-pack iPod headphones, these should be the headphones Apple offers with all iPods.

http://www.apple.com

Earbuds: Earjams, Griffin Technology, $14.95

While not headphones technically, these reasonably priced add-ons that mount to the stock Apple headphones offer a way to improve your lot without buying a completely new pair.

http://griffintechnology.com

Earbuds: MDR-EX71, Sony, $49.99

Comfortable, with great sound and rich bass, these headphones are a solid choice, and you won't have to shell out a ton of money. Available in white and black, these headphones should be near the top of everyone's list.

http://www.sonystyle.com

Behind-the-neck: MDR-G74SL, Sony, $39.99

These offer solid sound quality, a tangle-free cord, and easily the most comfy headphones this writer has ever blessed his head with. These are highly recommended if you're not into the earbud scene.

http://www.sonystyle.com

Over-the-head: TriPort Headpones, Bose, $149.99

If you're familiar with Bose, you know their reputation for quality. Take the Bose rep, throw in a hefty price tag for some very nice components, and you've got yourself one heck of a pair of cans. A little bulky for active iPod users, perhaps, but when quality is what matters most, these are a great option.

http://www.bose.com/

Wireless: Wireless Headphones for iPod, Logitech, $149.99

Logitech went a little kooky with this one, but they're still cool. They've created an accessory for your iPod or iPod Mini that allows it to broadcast audio to a wireless headset. This is the pinnacle of iPod freedom. Of course, the headphones won't work with anything but an iPod, so you'll have to be serious about your wireless freedom to justify the price.

http://www.logitech.com/

33

Stereo Docks

Sometimes headphones just don't cut it; you want to broadcast your iPod's audio like a "real" stereo. In this section, we'll take a look at your options in the realm of iPod stereo docks.

Though you can always simply run a cable from your iPod's Headphones/AC port to your stereo's audio input, there is a more elegant solution. Accessory makers are lining up to create portable stereos that feature built-in iPod docks. In addition to playing your tunes through powered, external speakers, these devices also act as charging stations for your iPod.

Choosing a stereo dock for your iPod can be a complicated process, as what appeals to you in a stereo is no doubt a very individual thing. Rather than making hard recommendations, we'll illustrate a few things you should look for when buying a stereo dock for your iPod, then show you a few models currently on the market to get your search rolling.

Nano users rejoice! Though your iPod is brand-spanking new, many of the docks on the market are already compatible with your iPod!

Frequency range: As with headphones, frequency range is important when purchasing speakers (of any kind). Generally, it's accepted that the human ear can process sound in the 20 to 20,000 Hz range. Speaker systems (whether their marketing provides this info or not) are always rated according to their possible frequency range. Look for stereo docks that cover the 20 to 20,000Hz range to ensure transparent sound reproduction with maximum clarity. The low end of that range (20 Hz) represents bass frequencies, so for those of you who prefer a full but un-muddied bass sound, make sure your system has the bottom end covered.

Power: Power, generally given in watts, isn't useful merely for demonstrating your coolness. Even if you don't intend to blast your speakers at your next block party, higher power levels often translate to better, cleaner sound at lower volumes. In short, you don't want to strain your speaker system, and more power makes this less likely. Of course, if you do want to shake the roof with your sound system, larger, more powerful speaker systems will do that, too.

Chapter 7

Speaker size: Bose is known for pushing the boundaries of physics; they make great-sounding stereos and speakers in small packages. Nevertheless, don't count physics out. If you want a nice, clear, thumping bass sound, bigger speakers are more equipped to handle the load. Though a well-designed stereo will almost always sound better than a poorly designed stereo (regardless of speaker size), this is one scenario is which size often matters.

Looks: Who are we kidding? Looks matter. The success of the iPod is almost certainly a result of the stunning designs Apple keeps coming up with. Perhaps the iPod Nano is the greatest expression of the allure of style when it comes to the MP3 player market—it's cool, and we all want it because it's cool. Why should your stereo be any different? The last thing you want to do is bring your Nano home to a stereo that belongs next to a group of aging breakdancers.

Listening test: The most important thing (other than price, perhaps) is how a stereo sounds to your ears. Forget what your friends say, forget what the Web says, and most definitely forget what the slack-jawed punk at your local electronics store says—your ears are the only ones that matter. Try as many stereos as you can before you buy, and follow your ears.

Recommended Stereo Docks

NOTE: Prices are current list prices at the time of this writing.

All iPods: Podwave, Macally, $39

Though it's not a speaker dock technically, the Podwave is perfect for those desiring external speakers with maximum portability. The Podwave is a battery-operated speaker set that plugs into your iPod's Headphones/AV port. The sound isn't as good as traditional speaker systems, but you won't find anything as portable as this. Use it on the road with your iPod's alarm function and you have the perfect alarm clock!

http://macally.com

All iPods with Dock Connector ports: SoundDock, Bose, $299

While it's far from portable, this monster of a speaker system brings richness and clarity that you might not believe. It even comes with a remote control. Truly a superb option, and it even looks as sharp as your iPod.

http://www.bose.com

All iPods with Dock Connector ports: OnStage, JBL, $160

Small but still lively, the JBL gives the Bose system a run for its money. This system is worth considering if you want the Bose but you also want to keep a chunk of change in your pocket.

http://www.jbl.com

All iPods with Dock Connector ports: iHome iH5, SDI, $100

A stereo/alarm clock, the iH5 is another stereo dock that was clearly designed with your sexy iPod in mind. Featuring robust alarm-clock features, full docking functionality, and quality sound, this a great choice for the price.

http://store.apple.com

Car Stereo Hookups

For anyone who drives—at all—the desire to play your iPod through your car stereo is almost religious in its intensity. In this section, we'll introduce the methods by which you can pipe your iPod through your car stereo system, then make some product recommendations.

Sadly, accessory makers have been very slow to market with devices that allow you to connect your iPod to your car stereo. As a result, there's a definite do-it-yourself vibe to the experience. Read on for a basic introduction to iPod-to-car connectivity.

Cassette adapters: If you still have a cassette deck in your, you're in luck! The same adapters that allow portable CD players to run through your car deck will work with any of the iPod models. These adapters feature a mock cassette at one end and stereo mini-plug at the other (which connects to your iPod's Headphones/AV port). Cassette adapters are dirt cheap, and they provide a hard-line connection to your stereo, which makes for excellent sound quality. Unfortunately, you need a tape deck in your car to use one, and these are becoming scarce.

FM transmitters: FM transmitters turn your iPod into your own personal radio tower. They connect to your iPod's Headphones/AV port and transmit a faint FM signal that can be tuned in by your car's FM receiver. Though they represent a step forward from cassette adapters technologically, this writer dislikes FM transmitters with a passion. To begin, they broadcast extremely weak radio signals; even if you're lucky enough to get a clean signal (interference from other radio broadcasts can be crippling), the audio is typically very poor. It isn't exactly fun if you've just shelled out for a new Nano and the thing sounds like a shortwave radio! If you have no other choice, there are two things you should look for in an FM transmitter: powered amplification (via an internal battery or car charger attachment) and a wide selection of frequency settings. The more frequency options your transmitter provides, the more likely you are to find the "secret" frequency that gives you a clear signal in your city.

Auxiliary input: Some car stereos feature auxiliary inputs so that external audio and video sources can be piped through your car's speakers. These inputs are usually at the back of the deck (i.e., hidden in your dash). If you have your stereo installer connect an audio cable to these inputs, then run the other end of the cable (with a stereo mini-plug) out through a hole in your dashboard, you've got yourself a hard-line connection for your iPod. Simply plug the stereo mini-plug into your iPod's Headphones/AV port, set your stereo to Aux In mode, and you're ready to rock. Granted, not everyone is going to want a cable hanging out of their dash permanently, but for this writer's money, this is the way to go; it maximizes the sound potential of your setup without going crazy on the money front.

iPod-ready decks and iPod adapters: Recently, deck manufacturers have—at last—recognized the need for full car stereo integration for iPod owners. Options currently come in several flavors: there are aftermarket car stereos that, when coupled with optional iPod adapters, work seamlessly with your iPod. Some of these will even charge your iPod and/or allow you to navigate through your playlists via your deck's controls. Another option is to buy a third-party adapter that allows you to connect your iPod to your stereo as if it were a CD changer (obviously, you'll need a deck with an available CD-changer port). The most exciting option, however, is reserved for those that are in the market for a new car. Some vehicle manufacturers are working with Apple to create car stereo systems that are designed from the ground up with your iPod in mind. These systems allow you to use your car itself as a docking station! A great summary of your options in this realm is available at Apple's Web site: http://www.apple. com/ipodnano/ipodyourcar/. Apple also provides a resource for those of us who aren't looking for new cars; see their site for a great rundown of aftermarket solutions: http://www.apple.com/ipodnano/ipodyourcar/ accessories.html.

Recommended Car Stereo Solutions

NOTE: Prices are current list prices at the time of this writing.

Car Cassette Adaptor, Macally, $14.99

If you have a tape deck in your car, this is the easiest (and cheapest) way to play your iPod through your car stereo. Plug the stereo mini-plug into your iPod, slip the tape adapter into your deck, and hit Play. It might not seem like much, but its sound is vastly superior to any FM transmitter on the market.

http://www.macally.com

iTrip family of FM transmitters, Griffin Technology, prices vary

With models for all iPods that have a Dock Connector and even a black unit to match the iPod U2 Special Edition, the iTrip is one of the better FM transmitters on the market. The range of frequencies it provides makes it a good choice for people in bigger cities, where radio stations tend to bleed in on one another. The iTrip Station Finder program (available through Griffin's Web site) can help you track down the best FM frequencies for your city. It's also handy when you're planning road trips!

http://www.griffintechnology.com

ice>Link Plus, Dension, $199.99

Dension's ice>Link Plus is an adapter that connects your iPod to your car stereo through a free CD-changer port. This technology offers a stepping stone between the "aux in" method described previously and a fully integrated iPod-ready stereo system. Dension's device provides the option of charging your iPod with the addition of an add-on accessory. It also allows for basic control of your iPod through your deck. There are restrictions, however: you'll need both a compatible vehicle and a compatible stereo deck. See Dension's Web site for details.

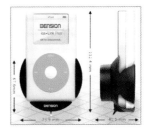

http://www.dension.com/

iPod-Ready head units, Alpine, prices vary

A bit spendy, but this is a great option if you're in the market for a new car stereo. Alpine has created a range of decks that are designed to offer iPod integration. Take one of these decks, add an optional adapter accessory, and you've got a seamless experience. You can charge your iPod and even navigate through its contents directly from your deck.

http://www.alpine-usa.com/driveyouripod/

35 Add-Ons and Upgrades

The iPod accessory market is out of control, and the options available are mind-blowing. These products simply make the experience of iPod ownership cooler, and often they add completely new functions to your player. We'll provide some of the highlights here to familiarize you with what your iPod can do when you venture into the accessories market.

Chapter 7

Recommended Add-Ons and Upgrades

NOTE: Prices are current list prices at the time of this writing.

iPods with color displays, excluding the iPod Nano: iPod Camera Connector, Apple, $29.00

Plug one end into your iPod, attach the other to your USB digital camera, and transfer photos from your camera's storage until you're blue in the face. (See Technique 27 for additional details.) This is a great way to reduce the need for a million flash cards when using your camera.

http://www.apple.com

All iPods w/ Dock Connector: Portable Charger for iPod, Solio, $99.95

How cool is this? It's a small, portable solar charger that you can use to charge your iPod. Easy to carry, highly efficient, and officially designated carbon neutral, this is great for charging your iPod anywhere the sun shines.

http://www.solio.com

iPods with Dock Connector, excluding iPod Mini and iPod Nano: Airclick, Griffin, $39.95

A wireless remote for your iPod that is easy to set up at home or in your car—mostly useful if you have your iPod connected to external speakers. Impressively, the Airclick uses RF signals rather than typical infrared signals. As a result, it will work through walls.

http://www.griffintechnology.com

All iPods: iSplitter, Monster, $12.95

Ever wish you could share your music with a friend, without having to hand over your headphones? With the iSplitter, you don't need to; plug both sets of headphones into it, plug its stereo mini-plug into your iPod, and make yourself a friend for life.

http://www.monstercable.com

iPods with Dock Connector, excluding iPod Mini and iPod Nano: Battery Pack for iPod, Belkin, $49.95

This battery pack, which operates on AA batteries, can power your iPod through its Dock Connector port. Attach it to your iPod like a backpack, and you're no longer tethered to a wall outlet. Not the most environmentally friendly option, but this is a solid choice for anyone who desires maximum portability. Campers take note!

http://www.belkin.com

iPods with Dock Connector: iFM Radio, Griffin, $49.99

Want to use your iPod as an FM radio? Now you can. Throw in a recording feature and remote control functions and you've got a nifty little gadget. Different iPods have different feature sets when using the iFM radio (e.g., the Mini and Nano lack recording capabilities). See Griffin's Web site for details.

http://www.griffintechnology.com

iPods with Dock Connector, excluding iPod Mini and iPod Nano: iTalk, Griffin, $39.95

Griffin's iTalk adds voice-recorder functionality to your full-size iPod. The recording quality is fairly poor due to limitations built into the iPod's firmware, but it still creates an exciting new use for your iPod. See Technique 19 for additional information related to recording voice memos.

http://www.griffintechnology.com

40 iPod Techniques

Maintenance and Troubleshooting

By now you're no doubt hooked on your iPod, and the thought of losing it to physical damage or software corruption horrifies your soul. Unfortunately, though the iPod is possibly the greatest thing ever, it is not the most impervious thing ever. Physically it's quite fragile, and—as is the case with all things that run software—it can fall victim to the occasional software glitch.

In Chapter 8 we'll discuss the best ways you can ensure a long, happy life for your iPod.

We'll also cover a variety of troubleshooting scenarios, just in case your iPod goes nutty on you.

36 Backing Up Your iPod

Chapter 8

One of the best things you can do to protect yourself from iPod disasters is to back up the contents of your iPod. We'll show you how.

Duplicating Your iPod's Contents

Some of the solutions to more severe iPod problems require that you delete the contents of your iPod. If you sync automatically, you've already got an operational backup for your iPod on your computer. However, even those using automatic sync are vulnerable if their computers (or hard drives) fail. Follow the steps given here to back up your iPod's contents.

1. Start by duplicating any non music files that you have on your iPod. With your iPod connected to iTunes, open your iPod preferences and select "Enable disk use" from the Music tab. Click OK.

2. With your iPod mounted to your computer as a drive, open its contents and select all the folders within—Calendars, Contacts, Notes, and Photos. Create a folder on your computer named "iPod Backup" and drag the folders from your iPod to it.

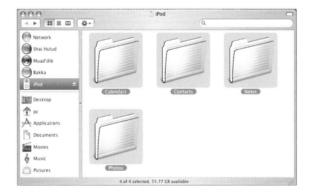

3. Now let's get your music. Open iTunes, bring up the iTunes preferences, select the Advanced tab, select the General tab (within Advanced), and note the location of your iTunes music folder. Now select the Consolidate Library command from the Advanced menu in

the menu bar. This will collect all the tracks in your library into the music library folder on your hard drive.

4. Delve into your computer's hard-drive directory and locate your iTunes music folder (based on your note from step 3). Right-click (or Ctrl-click) this folder and select the Copy command from the pop-up window. Open your iPod Backup folder, right-click (or Ctrl-click) in its contents window, and select the Paste command from the pop-up menu. This will duplicate your entire music library in this location. Note that these files cannot be transferred directly to your iPod (at least, not in a way that will allow you listen to them on your iPod). This is merely a means of backing up your library tracks in case anything happens to your library folder.

5. Now for your playlists! Enter iTunes, select a playlist, and choose Export Song List from the File menu. In the dialog box that pops up, select your iPod Backup folder as the destination. Repeat this step for each of your playlists.

6. You've now got your music library, your playlists, and all your data files stored in one handy location. You can either keep this folder on your hard drive or burn it to CD/DVD. Just remember to repeat this process periodically to keep your backup up to date.

estoring Your iPod's Contents

In the event that you acquire a new iPod or are forced to format yours as part of a troubleshooting procedure, you'll need to know how to restore its contents. If you've used automated syncing and you still have your source files on your computer (e.g., your iTunes library, calendars, contacts, notes, and photos), restoring the contents of your iPod is as simple as syncing it to your computer. iTunes will bring it up to date as if nothing happened (though it will take longer than usual). If you've lost this data, however, you can use a backup (stored on disc, perhaps) and the following procedure to get your iPod back in shape.

1. With your iPod enabled for disk usage, drag and drop the file folders from step 2 in the previous section (Calendars, Contacts, Notes, and Photos) from your iPod Backup folder directly to your iPod (mounted as a drive on

your desktop or in your My Computer directory). You'll receive a prompt asking if you wish to replace the existing folders on your iPod with your backup folders. Give the OK. Note that, although this restores your iPod's data files, these files will be deleted if you sync your iPod to your computer automatically. To avoid this, your must import your data files back into the folders or programs to which you're syncing your iPod. (For example, Mac users should import their calendars back into iCal.) See your software documentation for details. Also, remember that you will not be able to move photos back to your computer if you did not save full-resolution images to your iPod (using the full-resolution option on the Photos tab of your iPod preferences).

2. To rebuild your iTunes library, open iTunes and select Preferences from the iTunes (Mac) or Edit (PC) menu. Proceed to the General area of the Advanced tab and check the "Copy files to iTunes Music folder when adding to library" option. Click OK.

3. Drag and drop the library folder from your iPod Backup location into the iTunes Track frame. All of your audio will be copied into your iTunes music folder and added to your library. This may take some time, depending on how many tracks you have.

4. To import your playlists, select Import from the file menu and select a playlist from your iPod Backup location. Repeat this step for each of your playlists.

5. Now you need only sync your iPod to iTunes (or transfer tracks manually through iTunes, if you prefer) to bring it up to spec. See Chapter 1 for detailed instructions related to syncing.

37 Solutions for Common Problems

Though your iPod is your baby, it can throw tantrums from time to time. In Technique 37 we'll provide a grab bag of answers to some common problems.

Resetting Your iPod

If your iPod becomes unresponsive or doesn't turn on, check to make sure the Hold switch isn't activated. Slide the switch back and forth to double-check. If you're using a remote accessory, check to see that the remote isn't in Hold mode. Also, make sure your iPod is charged, of course. A dead battery makes for a dead iPod.

If nothing seems to fix the problem, reset your iPod. Your iPod very rarely shuts down in the way your computer does; instead, it simply goes to sleep when you turn it "off." Resetting your iPod effectively reboots its system software, not unlike rebooting your computer after a crash. Reset your iPod by pressing and holding the Menu and Select buttons for about six seconds, or until the Apple icon appears on the LCD screen.

General Troubleshooting

If your computer doesn't react when you connect your iPod

- First make sure you've installed the necessary software and drivers for both your iPod and your FireWire or USB 2.0 interface.

- Check to make sure the cable connection is secure; unplug the cable and plug it in again. Try an alternate FireWire or USB 2.0 port if one is available.

- If your iPod is not directly connected to your computer and is routed instead through a hub or another peripheral, try connecting your iPod directly to your computer, either via FireWire or USB 2.0.

- Try logging out of your system or user account, then logging back in.

- Restart your computer.

- Try completely draining your iPod's battery, then recharging it.

If your iPod will not play iTMS-purchased music

- Check to make sure your computer is authorized. If the Authorize Computer command appears in the Advanced menu of the iTunes menu bar, you must authorize your system prior to transferring songs to your iPod. You'll need your Apple or AOL login for this.

- If your computer is already authorized, deauthorize it and reauthorize it.

- Make sure your version of iTunes is up to date. Sometimes, new versions of iTunes will "break" the Digital Rights Management of previously purchased tracks. Note that iPod Nano users must have at least iTunes 4.9 to play iTMS songs on their players.

If your iPod won't play any music

- Make sure the Hold button isn't active.

- Make sure the Pause button isn't active and that the volume hasn't been turned all the way down.

- If you're using a dock, make sure your iPod is seated properly in it and that all connections are secure.

- If you're using a dock's Line Out port, make sure your external speakers and stereo are powered up and properly connected.

If you're using USB 2.0 for song and/or data transfer and it seems to be going slower than usual

- Check the status of your iPod's battery. If low, it will enter a power-saving mode. This results in slower data-transfer speeds. Detach your iPod and charge it for an hour or so, then reattempt the transfer.

- If the problem persists, try reinstalling the drivers for your USB 2.0 interface, then try a different USB cable.

If your iPod displays a folder with an exclamation mark

- Charge your iPod; the battery may be too low for the iPod to load its system software properly.
- Try updating your iPod's software using the iPod Updater application (installed when you install Apple's iPod software package).
- Reboot the iPod following the steps given previously. If the folder doesn't go away, charge your iPod and reboot again.
- If that still fails, you will need to restore your iPod (see Technique 38). Failing that, your iPod will require servicing.

If your iPod displays a battery with an exclamation mark

- Charge your iPod; make sure you use a working power source.
- Try resetting your iPod using the steps provided previously in this technique.
- Your battery might be kaput; if all else fails, contact Apple's customer support.

If your iPod displays a picture of a power adapter and a wall socket

- Plug your iPod into a wall socket through its power adapter!

If your iPod Shuffle seems dead

- Your Shuffle might be in Hold mode. If the status light blinks orange when you give a command, this is the case. Hold the Play/Pause button until the status light blinks green.
- Turn your Shuffle on and off.
- Try charging your Shuffle; you may have a dead battery.
- Restore your Shuffle using the instructions given in Technique 38.

38 Restoring Your iPod

When your iPod simply won't work and things start to look dire, it's time to restore your iPod to its factory settings. You'll also need to do this if you want to move a Mac-formatted iPod to a Windows PC. In this techique, we'll show you how.

1. Connect your iPod to your computer. Quit iTunes if you have it set to open automatically.

2. Open the iPod Updater program, making sure you have the latest version installed. (See the next technique to get instructions for updating your software.) By default, iPod Updater is installed in the [Startup Drive] > Applications > Utilities > iPod Updater Software folder on Macs, and in the C:\Program Files\iPod folder on Windows PCs.

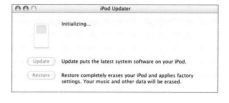

3. Once iPod Updater recognizes your iPod, click the Restore button. You'll get an alert message asking you to confirm your request. Your iPod will unmount from your computer during the restoration process, then reappear on your system once the process concludes.

The Restore option reverts your iPod to its original factory state; everything is deleted, including all your settings, audio tracks, and data files. If you experience problems with your iPod that general troubleshooting procedures don't take care of, the Update option (covered in our next technique) is a good place to start. Use the Restore option only if you're at a loss and the thought of deleting your songs bothers you less than the thought of your iPod living the rest of its life as a paperweight!

39

Keeping Your Software Up to Date

Keeping software up to date is critical for iPod users. Apple is always refining the way your iPod works, but you can't take advantage of these advancements if you don't update your software. In Technique 39 we'll show you how to quickly check for updates, then walk you through the installation process.

Apple is always tinkering with the software that runs your iPod. Every few months a new version of their iPod Updater program is released (for both Windows and Mac users). At a minimum, these updates fix bugs and allow your iPod to run more smoothly. Sometimes we iPod users get lucky, and software updates add features to our players or dramatically improve their operations. For example, one of Apple's previous updates provided for vastly more efficient battery usage, and iPod users everywhere were able to get hours of additional playback on each charge.

New versions of iTunes are also released regularly, and these almost always add new features that benefit iPod users. Recent iTurnes releases have brought powerful search functions, new audio encoding options, the ability to group playlists into folders, and a sexy new interface to the party.

Another benefit of updating your software is that it tends to alleviate troubleshooting concerns. Generally speaking, if your iPod is acting wacky, try a software update—often it does the trick.

Updating Software in Mac OS X

If you just bought your Mac, there's a very good chance all your software is preinstalled and up to date. Apple definitely wants you to hit the ground running with your iPod (or pave the way for you to buy one!). If you just bought your iPod, the software that came with it is also probably current, and you can refer to this book's Introduction for installation assistance. If neither of these scenarios is true for you, you'll need to be proactive about keeping your Mac's software up to date.

If you've set Mac OS X's Software Update feature to check for updates automatically, you'll be alerted to new versions of iPod Updater and iTunes and given the option of updating these programs automatically. If you'd like to know immediately whether your software is current, you can manually check for updates using Software Update.

1. Click the Apple menu at the upper left of your screen. Select the System Preferences option.

2. Click the Software Update icon in the System subsection.

3. Click the Check Now button in the Software Update window.

4. If any iPod- or iTunes-related software updates are available, select them and click the Install button. Follow the on-screen prompts to complete your updates.

5. Once you've updated both iPod Updater and iTunes, open the iPod Updater application to ensure the software on your iPod is current.

pdating Software in Windows

If you just bought your iPod, the software that came with it is probably current, and you can refer to this book's Introduction for installation assistance. Otherwise, the Windows version of iTunes offers a very easy way to check for new versions of iTunes; simply open the program and select Check For iTunes Updates from the Help menu at the top of the screen. iTunes will alert you if an update is available.

Consult Apple's Web site for updates to iPod Updater (http://www.apple.com/ipod/download/). Apple cleverly includes a date as part of the iPod Updater application name. As a result, recognizing newer versions of the program couldn't be easier.

hecking for Updates on the Web

Both Mac and PC users have the option of checking for software updates manually through Apple's Web site.

iPod Updater can be found at the iPod download page (www.apple.com/ipod/download/).

iTunes can be found at the iTunes download page (http://www.apple.com/itunes/download/).

Updating Your iPod's Software

When a new version of iPod Updater is released, follow these steps once you've installed the program to bring your iPod's software up to date.

1. Connect your iPod to your computer. If iTunes opens automatically, quit the program.

2. Open iPod Updater. By default, iPod Updater is installed in the [Startup Drive] > Applications > Utilities > iPod Updater Software folder on Macs, and in the C:\Program Files\iPod folder on Windows PCs.

3. Once your iPod is initialized, click the Update button and follow the on-screen prompts to complete the process.

Physical Care of Your iPod

For most people, the iPod (no matter which model you buy) represents a fairly expensive purchase. By virtue of its size and the high-tech nature of its components, the iPod is also fairly fragile. This combo makes for nervous iPod users! To close the book, we'll offer some tips for taking care of your iPod.

The various iPods are each made of very stylish materials. Unfortunately, these materials aren't exactly known for their resistance to scratching. The chrome back plates featured on the iPod and iPod Nano are particularly prone to disfigurement. The good news is that a cosmetic defect here and there hardly impedes your enjoyment of your iPod. It's still awesome and it still has a ton of music on it, so even those of us who pamper our iPods can usually learn to live with a few blemishes. Nevertheless, here are some tips for maximizing your iPod's youthful vigor:

Don't drop your iPod: A little obvious, yes, but also vital. Though your iPod should be used as part of an active lifestyle, try to minimize excessively perilous usage. iPods with hard drives (iPod and iPod Mini) are particularly vulnerable if they are dropped while their drives are being accessed; one solid drop and your iPod is a paperweight. Note that Apple's warranty will not cover user-inflicted destruction.

No swimming allowed: Your iPod is about as far from waterproof (or water-resistant) as you can get. Keep it away from liquids and sources of water. Yes, listening to "Der Kommissar" in the bathtub is great fun, but your iPod will hate you for it.

Get a case: See Technique 31 for the skinny on cases. Obviously, the best way to protect your iPod is to encase it in something that will bear the brunt of your abuse. In particular, look for something that covers your screen (in addition to the rest of your iPod). Your screen is the one place where scratches will drive you batty because you'll have to look at them every time you use your iPod.

Watch your ins and outs: The most delicate areas of your iPod are its inputs and outputs. Many of the cases on the market effectively cover these ports, thus ensuring you won't fill them with dirt or your favorite flavor of soda. Whether you have such a case or not, be aware that everything on your iPod comes in through its Dock Connector port (or USB connector, in the case of the Shuffle); if it's stuffed full of cheese curds you won't be able to sync very well. Shuffle users should, of course, always employ their USB caps whenever their iPod isn't connected to their computer.

Use a soft, lint-free, non-abrasive cloth: Pick up a kit for cleaning glasses and sunglasses. These often contain a wiping cloth that will work brilliantly on your iPod's surface—including its screen. Blow on your iPod prior to wiping it down; this will remove dust and other tiny particles that might scratch your iPod's finish as you wipe it down.

Do not use cleaners of any kind: Don't use solvents meant for your kitchen sink on your precious iPod! Lightly dampen your cleaning cloth with good old H_2O if your iPod is stubbornly besmirched. Make sure you avoid getting moisture into any of your iPod's openings—Dock Connector ports do not like liquid! When using a dampened cloth, be sure to unplug and power off your iPod, just to play it safe.

Watch your temp: As we've discussed earlier, your iPod prefers room temperature. This isn't to say it will explode in your hands if you venture outside, but—in general—try to store your iPod in a comfy climate. Your iPod's battery, in particular, is highly vulnerable to high temperatures, so refrain from leaving it in your car on hot days.

Do not attempt internal repairs: Unless you're a mad genius, it's safe to assume you won't be able to solve any problems by cracking your iPod open. More importantly, the second you attempt this, Apple sends your warranty through a shredder. If your iPod seems to have died on you, read your warranty and contact Apple's customer support.

We all scream for Ice Creme: If your iPod is severely scratched up, consider the Ice Creme v.2 scratch remover kit from Radtech. It's designed and marketed for the iPod, and the Ice Creme kit has a solid reputation in the iPod community. Check it out at Radtech's Web site: http://www.radtech.us/.

40 iPod Techniques

The Fifth-Generation iPod and iTunes 6

There's late-breaking news! As this book was going to press, Apple launched yet another revolutionary iPod model: the fifth-generation (5G) iPod. The 5G model offers several advancements over the 4G iteration, but one stands out: support for video playback. In Chapter 9 (our "bonus" chapter), we'll introduce the new iPod and its operations (where they differ from other iPod models). We'll also introduce the new features and operations of iTunes 6.

iPod Advancements

The 5G iPod offers a slew of advancements over previous models. The unit is thinner, lighter, and comes in two colors—black and white. It also sports five additional hours of battery life. In comparison to previous models, the display is massive: 2.5 inches. Why? Because, though it may not be the "Video iPod" rumor sites and forum dwellers have been guessing about for years, it does play videos—quite sexily, in fact. Perhaps best of all, the lower-priced model (though it shares the fourth-generation, 20 GB iPod's price tag) clocks in at 30 GB. And you thought you wouldn't have room for those big, fat video files!

Feature Comparison and Basic Operations

The 5G iPod shares most of the features we all know and love from the 4G iPod, iPod Nano, and iPod Mini. Though thinner and lighter, the hardware is very similar to the 4G iPod, with the notable exception of the iPod Remote port, which has been removed. (This port was also excluded from the iPod Nano.)

With the exception of its unique, video-related functions, the unit's menu navigation matches that of the iPod Nano. Yes, that means the iPod is no longer bereft of the World Clock, Stopwatch, and Screen Lock features introduced by the iPod Nano.

In a nutshell, the iPod operations covered elsewhere in this book still apply—from the device's controls to its software operations. Refer to the techniques throughout this book for detailed explanations of all the 5G iPod's "legacy" functions.

Few Things to Note...

For select operations, the different iPod models behave differently. In short, some of the things that work on certain models don't work on other models. The list below covers where the 5G iPod stands on these issues:

FireWire operations: As with the Nano, you can charge the new iPod via FireWire, but you cannot transfer files to it using a FireWire connection.

TV-out functionality: Yes, the new iPod offers this option (with the support of the iPod AV Cable)! The Nano might not do this, but your 5G iPod can. See Technique 26 for instructions related to piping your iPod through a TV.

Direct-from-camera photo transfers: Using the iPod Camera Connector, you can transfer images to your iPod directly from your digital camera (or memory-card reader). The iPod Nano doesn't allow this, but (thankfully) this limitation does not apply to its big brother. See Technique 27 for instructions related to this function.

Recording voice memos: You can do this, too! You'll need a microphone accessory, of course, but this function hasn't been abandoned by Apple. See Technique 19 for details.

PC/Mac: The Shuffle offers its owners complete cross-platform freedom, but the new iPod is governed by the same rules as the rest of its family. If you format it on a PC it will work on a Mac, but if you format it on a Mac you'll need to reformat it before you can use it on a PC. There is one way around this: get yourself a third-party application that will "translate" when you connect your Mac-formatted iPod to a PC. (See the entry for XPlay in Technique 21 for one such program.)

Unique 5G iPod Operations

Though the new iPod has a lot in common with its older siblings, Apple just wouldn't be Apple if they didn't throw some new stuff into the mix. In this section we'll cover the operational differences between the 5G iPod and the rest of the gang.

Lyrics

Before we get into the real nitty-gritty of the new iPod (i.e., video), we should mention that the 5G iPod brings another cool feature to the iPod palette: you can now view lyrics as you listen to tracks on your iPod. To view lyrics on your iPod, simply click the Select button repeatedly from the Now Playing screen until the lyrics appear. The lyrics will scroll as the song plays.

Note that you must add lyrics to your audio files in order to view them on your iPod. We'll cover the procedure for adding lyrics to your files (using iTunes 6 or later) a bit later in this chapter.

Viewing Videos on Your iPod

Naturally, the most exciting feature of the 5G iPod is its ability to play videos. Play videos on your iPod much like you would music:

1. Select Videos from the main menu.

2. Browse through your video collection, then initiate and control playback just as you would for an audio track. You can also select videos from the Music menu. However, if you play a video from this menu, your iPod will play the audio for only the selected file.

Viewing iPod Videos on Your TV

Play your iPod's videos through a TV just as you would a photo slideshow. See Technique 26 for instructions. The new iPod does have one unique function in this respect, however: since many of the videos you'll be watching on your iPod are in the widescreen format, the iPod now offers an option for switching between widescreen and full-screen playback on your TV. Toggle this option from the Videos > Video Settings menu.

Filling Your iPod with Videos

Of course, you can't view videos on your iPod before you've moved them there! Fortunately, the procedures for transferring video files to your iPod are the same as those for transferring songs. There's nothing new to learn! See Chapter 1 for all the details related to track transfers, track info, and playlists.

As for getting your hands on videos suited to your iPod, Apple has made that easy: a variety of videos can be purchased from the iTunes Music Store. (We'll cover this in greater detail in the next section.)

Another option is to prepare your own videos for playback on your iPod. This is possible, but a few restrictions apply. First off, your iPod can play videos only in the QuickTime and MPEG-4 formats: .mov, .m4v, and .mp4. (in other words, the native formats of Apple's QuickTime software). So you'll need to capture or convert your videos to compatible formats if you wish to view them on your iPod. Generally, this means using Apple's QuickTime Pro (Mac or PC) or iMovie (Mac only) to prepare your video files. Alternatively, you can export to QuickTime formats from some third-party programs.

New in iTunes 6

Released very soon after the debut of iTunes 5 (which marked a major advancement in the iTunes program), iTunes 6 adds a few features designed to integrate with the 5G iPod's special features.

Adding Lyrics to Audio Tracks

To embed lyrics in a track (for viewing on your iPod during playback), select the desired track and right-click (or Ctrl-click). Select Get Info from the pop-up menu. From the Get Info dialog box, select the Lyrics tab. Type or paste lyrics into the text field and click OK. That's all there is to it!

▲ Entering lyrics in the Get Info dialog box

Opening the Video Viewer Frame

The first thing you'll want to do when you start exploring videos in iTunes is open the Video Viewer frame. If you've worked with album artwork in the past, you no doubt already have this open. If not, click the "Show or hide song artwork or video viewer" button at the lower left of your iTunes window (the fourth button over from the left) to bring up the viewer. Videos played in iTunes will be displayed here. Click and drag the right edge of the viewer frame to alter the size of the video display.

▲ Opening the Video Viewer frame

Browsing Video Files

iTunes 6 brings a new entry to the Source list: Videos. Select the Videos listing to view the videos in your iTunes library. At the top of the Videos view you'll notice a bar similar to the Search bar that appears when you search for keywords in your library. Use these buttons (Movies, Music Videos, Podcasts, TV Shows, etc.) to aid your browsing. Use the buttons at the upper left of the Videos view (just under the Browse button) to select your preferred method for browsing through your videos—either a text list (similar to the view shown when browsing audio tracks) or thumbnail layout.

▲ Selecting Videos from the Source list

Editing Video Info

Once you've selected a video file, you can edit its embedded information just as you would an audio file, with one notable difference: the Lyrics tab is grayed out in the Get Info dialog box. (Not surprisingly, Apple didn't think it would be necessary to embed lyrics in video files.)

Playing Videos

With a video selected (and the Video Viewer frame open), play the video as you would any audio track. By default, the video will play in the Video Viewer frame. When a video is playing in this frame, a fifth button appears just below the Video Viewer frame. Click the "Show videos or visuals full screen" button to do just that.

Click the Video Viewer frame once to launch the video in its own window. From this dedicated window, you can resize the video, control playback, and adjust the playback volume. Note that volume adjustments made in the pop-up video window will translate to iTunes' main volume control.

▲ The pop-up video window

Downloading Videos from the iTunes Music Store

Though you can transfer your own videos to your iPod (provided they're in a supported QuickTime format), this doesn't necessarily mean you've got any videos on your hard drive that you'd want to watch on your iPod! Enter the iTunes music store.

The easiest way to load your iPod with quality videos, not surprisingly, comes with a price tag. Apple offers an assortment of video files for download at $1.99 a pop. These can be purchased through the iTMS just like songs. To browse the videos on offer, go the iTMS homepage and select Music Videos, Pixar, or TV Shows from the Inside the Music Store navigation menu. (In the Pixar area you'll find a selection of animated shorts from Steve Jobs's other hugely successful company.) It's certain that the number of categories—and the selections within each category—will grow.

▲ Browsing the TV shows on offer at the iTMS

Another great option for acquiring video files comes courtesy of a familiar friend: podcasts. The technology for video podcasts has been around for a while now; we simply lacked the iPod to play them. Not so anymore! Podcasts with embedded video are now popping up all over the place.

You can access these either from the Podcasts listing in the Source list (click the Podcast Directory button at the bottom of the screen) or the Podcasts area of the iTMS. Use the same procedures (covered in Technique 14) for video podcasts that you would for audio podcasts. To assist in your browsing, a small television icon appears to the right of podcasts that include video content. Note that video podcasts will appear in both the Videos and Podcasts areas of the iTunes Source list.

Index

A

AAC Library, 55
AAC (MP4)
audio, 20
accessories, 119–136
  add-ons and upgrades, 134–136
  car stereo hookups, 131–133
  cases, 120–123
  headphones, 124–127
  stereo docks, 128–130
add-ons, 134–136
Airclick, 135
alarm clock, 74
Anapod Explorer, 88
artwork, track, 40
Audible.com, 62
audio
  collection, expanding, 57–69
  formats, 19–20
  free, 68–69
  importing from CD, 22–23
  importing from hard drive, 21
  transcoding, 53–55
  transfer, manual, 49–50
  transfer, to another computer, 94–95
  troubleshooting, 144
audiobooks
  Audible.com purchase, 62
  iTMS purchase, 61–62
  use on iPods, 63
Autofill feature (iPod Shuffle), 114
automatic sync, 45–46
  defined, 45
  initiating, 45
  on-the-go playlists, 52
  semi-, 47–48

B

backups, 140–142
battery
  charging, 28
  display with exclamation mark, 145
  drain, reducing, 27
  memory cache and, 28
  storage, 26
Battery Pack for iPod, 135
Book2Pod, 86

C

calendars
  events, adding (Mac), 78–79
  events, adding (Windows), 79
  events, viewing on iPod, 80
  workarounds, 80
cameras, iPod with, 105–106
Car Cassette Adaptor, 132
care, iPod, 151–152
car stereo hookups, 131–133
  auxiliary input, 131–132
  cassette adapters, 131
  FM transmitters, 131
  recommended, 132–133
cases, 120–123
  cooling, 120
  dock interference, 121
  iPod Nano Tubes, 122
  iPod Socks, 121
  iSkin, 123
  leather, 123
  materials, 120–121
  recommended, 121–123
  screen protection, 120
  Sleevz for iPod, 122
  SV iMini, 122
cassette adapters, 131
CDs, importing audio from, 22–23
Click Wheel, 9, 29, 34
clock, 34, 72–74
  alarm, 74
  computer clock sync, 72
  iPod/iPod Mini, 72–73
  iPod Nano, 73–74
  sleep timer, 74
connecting iPod, 35–36
contacts, 75–77
  adding (Mac), 75–76
  adding (Windows), 76–77
  vCard format, 77
  viewing, on iPod, 77
Contacts menu, 34
contents
  duplicating, 140–141
  iPod, 46
  manual management, 49
  restoring, 141–142
cross-platform disk usage, 93

D

date and time, 34
Digital Rights Management (DRM), 60
disconnecting iPod, 36
displays, troubleshooting, 145

E

earbuds, 125–126
Earjams, 126
editing
  track info, 37–39
  track preferences, 39–40
  video info, 160
Equalizer presets, 39

F–G

fifth-generation (5G) iPod, 155–159
  advancements, 156
  feature comparison, 156–157
  lyrics, 157
  operations, 157–158
  video, 158–159
FireWire operations, 156
FM transmitters, 131
folders
  Calendar, 79
  with exclamation mark, 145
  iTunes music, 141
  photo, syncing to, 99
  playlists in, 43–44
free music, 68–69

H

hard drives
  cross-platform usage, 93
  importing audio from, 21
  iPods as, 92–93
headphones, 124–127
  comfort, 124
  cords, 125
  Earjams, 126
  frequency range, 124
  In-Ear Headphones, 125
  MDR-EX71, 126

MDR-G74SL, 126
packaged with iPods, 124
portability, 125
ports, 30
recommended, 125–127
TriPort, 127
Wireless Headphones for
iPod, 127
Hold button, 30

I–K
iCal (.ics) file format, 79, 80
ice>Link Plus, 133
iFM Radio, 136
iHome iH5, 130
image formats, 98
importing audio, 19–23
from CD, 22–23
from hard drive, 21
In-Ear Headphones, 125
iPod Camera Connector, 134
iPod It, 87
iPod Mini, 9
iPod Nano, 9, 10
screen lock, 84–85
stopwatch, 83–84
iPod Nano Tubes, 122
iPod Photo, 9
iPods
buying, 10–11
connecting/disconnecting,
35–36
generations, 7, 8–9
physical care, 151–152
as portable hard drive, 92–93
iPod Shuffle, 9, 109–117
advanced operations,
113–115
Autofill feature, 114
disk storage, 116–117

file transfer, 116–117
as flash drive, 116–117
hardware, 110–111
manual transfers, 114
operations, 112
overview, 109
playing, 112
plugging in, 113
preferences, 115
troubleshooting, 112, 145
iPod Skins, 123
iPod Socks, 121
iPodSync, 88
iPod U2 Special Edition, 9
iPod Updater, 13
iSkin cases, 123
iSpeak, 87
iSplitter, 135
iTalk, 136
iTrip FM transmitters, 133
iTunes
buttons, 17–19, 36
defined, 13
getting started, 16–23
importing audio in, 19–23
installation, 13–15
library, 37–40, 55, 94–95, 142
for Mac OS X, 12
menus, 16–17
playlists, 41–44
Setup Assistant, 21, 35
Source list,
46, 55, 92, 99, 113, 115
user interface, 16
version 6, 159–161
video viewer, 159
for Windows, 11, 12
iTunes Music Store (iTMS)
account creation, 59–60
audiobook purchases, 61–62

music, troubleshooting, 144
navigating, 58–59
podcasts, 64–65
storefront, 58
track samples, 59
videos, 158, 161

L
LCD screen, 29
leather cases, 123
library
adding music to, 55
organizing, 37–40
rebuilding, 142
transferring to another
computer, 94–95
Lossless audio formats, 19
lossy audio formats, 19
lyrics, 157, 159

M
Macs, 11, 12–13
calendar events, adding,
78–79
contacts, adding, 75–76
cross-platform disk usage, 93
photo application syncing, 98
software installation, 14
third-party software, 86–87
updating software with,
148–149
**manual operation, 49–50, 52,
114**
MDR-EX71 earbuds, 126
MDR-G74SL headphones, 126
menus
iPod, 31
iTunes, 16–17

N
Next/Fast-forward button, 31
notes, 81

O
OnStage, 130
on-the-go playlists, 51–52

P–Q
photos, 97–107
application syncing (Mac), 98
application syncing
(Windows), 99
folder, syncing, 99
full-resolution, 100
image formats, 98
imported, viewing, 106
slideshows, viewing, 101–102
transfer, from camera,
105–106
transfer, from iPod to
computer, 100
viewing, manually, 101
viewing, on iPod, 101–102
viewing, on TV, 103–104
playback operations, 30–31
Play button, 30
playlists
creating, 41–44
deleting, 42
dumb, 41–42
in folders, 43–44
importing, 142
on-the-go, 51–52
renaming, 41
smart, 42–43, 47
transferring, to another
computer, 95
Pod2Go, 86

podcasts
defined, 64
finding, 64–65
on iPod, 67
listening, in iTunes, 66
removing, 66
transfer, to iPod, 67
PodPlus, 87
Podwave, 129
Portable Charger for iPod, 134
portable storage devices,
116–117
purchasing, 10–11

R

Remote port, 30
Repeat mode, 32
resetting iPod, 143
restoring
contents, 141–142
iPod, 146

S

screen lock, 84–85
Select button, 29, 31
semi-automatic sync, 47–48
on-the-go playlists, 52
uses, 47, 48
Senuti, 86
settings, customizing, 32–34
Setup Assistant, 21, 35
Shuffle mode, 32
skins, 123
Sleep Timer option, 74
Sleevz for iPod, 122
slideshows
viewing on iPod, 101–102
viewing on TV, 104
smart playlists, 42–43, 47

software
installation, 13–15
Mac, 86–87
third-party, 86–88
updating, 26, 147–150
Windows, 87–88
SoundDock, 130
Source list (iTunes),
46, 55, 92, 99, 113, 115
stereo docks
characteristics, 128–129
recommended, 129–130
selecting, 128
stopwatch, 83–84
SV iMini, 122

T

third-party software, 86–88
tracks
AAC, 55
artwork, 40
drag and drop, 49
DRM, 60
Equalizer presets, 39
info, editing, 37–39
iTMS, 59
lyrics, 159
preferences, editing, 39–40
rating, 39
transcoding audio, 21, 53–55
process, 53–55
support, 53
warning, 53
TriPort headphones, 127
troubleshooting, 143–145
TV
connecting to, 103–104
out functionality, 157
signal options, 104
viewing slideshows on, 104

viewing videos on, 158

U

updating software, 147–150
benefits, 147
iPod, 150
in Mac OS X, 148–149
on the Web, 149
in Windows, 149
upgrades, 134–136

V

vCard format, 75, 77
videos
downloading from iTMS, 161
files, browsing, 160
info, editing, 160
iTunes viewer, 159
playing, 160
viewing, on iPod, 158
viewing, on TV, 158
voice memos, 82, 157
volume, changing, 30

W

Windows, 11
calendar events, adding, 79
contacts, adding, 76–77
cross-platform disk usage, 93
photo application syncing, 99
software installation, 15
third-party software, 87–88
updating software with, 149
**Wireless Headphones for
iPod,** 127

X–Z

XPlay, 88